Attempted Suicide

THE ESSENTIAL GUIDEBOOK FOR LOVED ONES

Juliet Kirwan Carr

Juliet Kirwan Carr lives in Colorado with her husband, three children, and an assortment of rescue animals. She has lived through two suicide attempts by her father, numerous suicide attempts by other family members and friends, as well as suicide deaths. She has endured suicidal thinking herself. You can learn more about coping with a suicide attempt, and how to prevent suicide, in your family or community at _AttemptedSuicideHelp.com_.

Cover Artwork: Teddi Roy

Cover Design: Katie Anderson

Photo Credit: Mike Boese at Peak Life Photography

Introduction

I began thinking about writing this book after my father's first suicide attempt. After his attempt, I had searched unsuccessfully for some tool – a book, Website, support group, or brochure – to help me feel validated, supported, less confused. I had questions. I was afraid. I felt alone, as though I was the only person who ever experienced the tragedy of a suicide attempt in her family. I would have been happy with anything that provided any answers. The Internet held vast resources for people bereaved by suicide – those left behind after a suicide death – but nothing for people in my position.

After my father's second attempt at suicide, I plunged deeper into despair, wallowing alone in my own grief and confusion. Every phone call made me wonder if I was going to learn about his third attempt and a possible suicide completion. I was riddled with terror, anxiety, post-traumatic stress disorder (PTSD), lack of sleep, lack of understanding, and lack of support.

At the time, I wondered, "Will I feel better?" "When will I quit crying?" "My kids are great; my husband is great. Why can't I feel better?" As I emerged from a two-year mental fog, the idea of writing this book became more concrete and provided me with a purpose.

I wanted others who found themselves in the role of family member or friend of someone who had attempted suicide, but not completed, to have something they could hold, touch, dog-ear, highlight, underline, and share. I hoped they might feel a sense of belonging and courage in this unique community they didn't join willingly, but were thrust into. I wanted to provide answers.

I also wanted a guidebook for friends of people in this attempt-survivor community, so they could offer their understanding and support. My friends had no idea what to say or do to help me. I wanted them to know, but I didn't know what to tell them when I was in the middle of my grief.

This book gives you glimpses into what it feels like to be the loved one of a suicide attempt survivor. You will read quotes from people who are angry, mistrustful, and frustrated. You will read quotes from people who have moved on, found joy in their lives, and continue to love. There simply are no right or wrong feelings and thoughts. The quotes are included with the hope you may find a few words or phrases that feel familiar, or things you have thought or said. This familiarity may help you realize you are not alone.

"I actually thought that I was going crazy." That is how one of my interviewees felt. He finally realized, "No, this is normal. You are not going crazy. You are grieving." And what a remarkable first step that was toward recovery. Indeed, you are not going crazy. You too, are grieving.

My wish is that this book will help you feel validated, encouraged, stronger, and understood. I want you to use this to make it through the difficult time that it takes you to return to "good" knowing others have gone before you and having the information it is possible.

All my best to you,
Juliet Kirwan Carr

This book is dedicated to all the brave, and maybe not so brave, people who are living with the reality of a suicide attempt and to the time in life when things will once again be good. Here is to being healthy.

Preface

There are as many situations surrounding suicide attempts as there are attempts. There isn't a magic reason or a one-size-fits-all solution. Because, at the time of my father's attempts, my experiences were the only ones I knew, I looked for information from others who also had family members or friends who attempted suicide to learn from these "experts". I wanted to know how their experiences were similar to mine and to each other's and I also wanted to understand how they were different.

Throughout this book, you will read some of their quotes.

If you are a loved one of a suicide attempter the notable quotes may help provide a sense of normalcy. You will read research from experts in the field of mental health and suicide prevention. Finally, you will read steps you can take to work your way back to what will be your new "normal life". It will not be exactly what you knew before the attempt, but it just might help you live a better life now and encourage you to make it better than it was before. It is possible.

If you are the friend of someone who has had an attempt in the family, I hope this book helps you to find the right words to say and the right actions to take as you continue to nourish your friendship.

I interviewed 33 people. They were parents, spouses, siblings, cousins, aunts, uncles, friends, and co-workers of those who attempted suicide, and people who attempted suicide themselves. Their ages ranged from mid-20s to mid-70s. Their experiences make up this book. Names and other identifying characteristics have not been included to protect people's privacy.

The single commonality that every person I interviewed shared: They all looked for a Website, book, or support groups to help them cope with the suicide attempt of a loved one. They found that there were few, if any, specific resources available for working through the feelings, questions, and circumstances surrounding an attempt.

As this book developed, so did a pattern – the stages of coping with an attempted suicide mirrored the stages of grief. Perhaps discussing an attempted suicide, which is often considered taboo within the context of what many consider the "normal" grieving process, will help to break through the stigma surrounding suicide attempts, as well.

Contents

This book is not meant to replace the help you can receive from professional therapy, counseling or doctors. If you are feeling suicidal or know someone who is, please call 1-800-273-8255. The information given is meant to help you through your grief process and back to wellness. Please seek professional help in addition to using this book as a tool in your tool box.

Background and Statistics

Background

hen I asked my interviewees how they felt after the suicide attempt of their loved one, answers included:

- I felt shock and anger
- I felt like I was in a coma
- I felt catastrophic and crazy
- Scattered and shattered
- Helpless
- I felt I was in a vacuum - unable to settle down, find peace, or closure
- I was unable to move forward, unable to complete this chapter of my life
- I felt a complete loss of control, security, and trust
- I was just waiting for it to happen again
- I lost my life, or what I thought my life was

I, too, felt all of this. And I desperately wanted to find someone else who felt the same way. I wanted to feel normal. I wanted to know that my thoughts, feelings and actions, belonged somewhere. But a suicide attempt is not the same as other losses. I wondered: "How do I live with these feelings when I have nowhere to turn? I have no one to talk to and know no one else who feels like I do, except for my family members and I don't want to victimize them."

When people think of grief they think of death, or a loss that makes it impossible to get back to how things were before. When someone dies, you are allowed to grieve. When a home burns down, you are allowed to grieve. When a marriage ends in divorce, you are allowed to grieve. When you lose a job, you are allowed to grieve.

But when someone you love attempts suicide, there is an expectation that you will get back to business quickly. Move forward. You do not grieve. After all, other people assume there has been no loss.

Things I was told:
- "Your dad is still alive, when are you going to get over it?"
- "You don't know what I would give to have just one more day with my brother. You are ungrateful."
- "No one died, so what is your problem?"
- "You should be thankful/grateful your dad is alive."
- "People who have a loved one attempt suicide do not grieve. If their loved one is diagnosed with a mental illness they grieve, but not if someone attempts suicide."
- "You should not be doing this work. You do not understand suicide. You should be doing everything you can to keep your father alive. You will regret this."

These are things I was told. Because of this I tried like hell to move on. I discounted my feelings, my thoughts, and my grief process because no one said it was healthy

6

or acceptable for me to grieve. No one understood that I had suffered a loss or validated that loss. Now I understand there is a loss, a big loss. This is a loss that is difficult to understand unless you live through it.

Think of it like this. You built a house with your hands and then discovered that the walls are filled with mold. The mold is suffocating you slowly. There is no insurance to help you rebuild, and your friends don't feel the tightness you feel when you breathe because they don't live there. You must tear the house down, board by board, by yourself, with no support – either emotional or financial – and you must replace each board with new, healthy wood at your own expense of time, money, and effort. And you do this alone. And you always wonder, "Will this new wood last?" This is what it feels like when you live with someone who has attempted suicide. Tightness of breath, wondering, questioning, afraid of more pain and loss.

I asked Carla Blowey, Dream Work Facilitator, author and grief specialist, about the grief process pertaining to suicide attempters and their loved ones. Her response was, "Yes, I do think those people grieve, but I don't think they know that grieving is what they are doing. People who have someone they love attempt suicide are grieving loss. There is a loss of a dream. There is a loss of hope, the loss of certainty of having relied on my life being a certain way. There is a belief that 'I did all

7

these things right so why is this happening to me?' I don't think they realize grieving is a legitimate response to what they are going through. Some people may think there is no permanence to a suicide attempt so (loved ones) have no reason to grieve. I do not believe that is true though." (Blowey, 2013)

When I asked Licensed Professional Counselor (LPC), Anna Adams, she stated, "I think a lot of people do work through the five stages of grief, or loss and don't realize that is what they are doing. A couple of examples of what they grieve, or have lost, are; the image/impression of the attempter and the changes in the relationship between them as a result of the attempt." (Adams, 2017)

It took me six years of living and researching and while discussing this with others someone said, "Maybe all loved ones of suicide attempters grieve." She helped me have the "Ah-Ha moment" – that moment when I realized that I did grieve. I grieved big time. So, ever hopeful with this realization, I did an Internet search for the word grief.

The first website listed was helpguide.org, and here is the information provided:

"Losing someone or something you love or care deeply about is very painful.

You may experience all kinds of difficult emotions and it may feel like the pain and sadness you're experiencing will never let up.

These are normal reactions to a significant loss. But while there is no right or wrong way to grieve, there are healthy ways to cope with the pain that, in time, can renew you and help you move on." (Melinda Smith, 2017)

And I realized that perhaps I could use my grief to strengthen and enrich my life. And, perhaps I could help others. To do that I had to express and experience my grief honestly and authentically, and you must also. Don't be afraid; many others have quietly and privately expressed and experienced this specific grief.

This guidebook is written to help you express and experience your own grief process, and then strengthen and enrich your own life.

What is grief?
Grief is a natural response to loss. It's the emotional suffering you feel when something or someone you love is taken away. You may associate grief with the death of a loved one – and this type of loss does often cause the

most intense grief. But any loss can cause grief – the end of a relationship, a change in health, loss of financial stability, loss of a dream, loss of safety. The more significant your loss, the more intense your grief will be.

"Grief confuses, exhausts, seems to block the mind from thinking." (Price, 1983)

When I asked Erik Cooper, Licensed Marriage and Family Therapist (LMFT), what he thought families who had survived a suicide attempt have lost or have the right to grieve his response was, "They have lost and are grieving the sacredness of their relationships. They have lost the heart-to-heart connections. They may have lost the ability to be sensitive to the attempters' emotions and needs. They are grieving the loss of connecting with the attempter on a sacred level. The loss is what they believe the future was going to be. They are grieving the loss of the closeness." (Cooper, 2012)

Everyone grieves differently
How you grieve depends on many factors. These include your personality and coping style, your life experience, your faith, the people surrounding

10

*supporting, loving and allowing you to grieve, and the nature of the loss. Healing happens gradually; it can't be forced or hurried – and **there is no "normal" timetable for grieving.** Grieving can last for days, weeks or years. You may think you have finished grieving and something strikes a nerve and you are steeped in grief again.*

I was struck that in all my research at libraries, online, in book stores, and in talking to people including professionals, grief included the loss of pets, jobs, relationships, homes, marriages, health, friends and even dreams, but none included a suicide attempt as a reason to grieve.

Was I the only person who came so unhinged about a suicide attempt? I did more research with the thought, "There must not be that many suicide attempts. People must complete suicide with nearly every attempt because there is a lot of support for those who are bereaved by suicide and nothing for people like me." Research proved me wrong.

Statistics

Per the National Institute of Mental Health: "Suicide is a major public health concern. Suicide is among the leading causes of death in the United States. Based on recent nationwide surveys, suicide in some populations is on the rise.

- **Suicide** is defined as death caused by self-directed injurious behavior with intent to die as a result of the behavior.
- A **suicide attempt** is a non-fatal, self-directed, potentially injurious behavior with intent to die as a result of the behavior. A suicide attempt might not result in injury.
- **Suicidal ideation** refers to thinking about, considering, or planning suicide.

Suicide is a Leading Cause of Death in the United States

Per the Centers for Disease Control and Prevention (CDC), in 2014:

- Suicide was the tenth leading cause of death overall in the United States, claiming the lives of more than 42,000 people.
- Suicide was the second leading cause of death among individuals between the ages of 10 and 34.

- There were more than twice as many suicides (42,773) in the United States as there were homicides (15,809).

Suicide Rates and Trends over Time

- Suicide rate is based on the number of people who have died by suicide per 100,000 population. Because changes in population size are taken into account, rates allow for comparisons from one year to the next.
- Over the past 15 years, the total suicide rate has increased 24% from 10.5 to 13.0 per 100,000.
- The suicide rate among males has remained approximately four times higher (20.7 per 100,000 in 2014) than among females (5.8 per 100,000 in 2014).
- Among females, the suicide rate was highest for those aged 45-64 (9.8 per 100,000).
- Among males, the suicide rate was highest for those aged 75 and over (38.8 per 100,000).
- The rates of suicide were highest for males (27.4 per 100,000) and females (8.7 per 100,000) in the American Indian/Alaska Native group, followed by males (25.8 per 100,000) and females (7.5 per 100,000) in the White/non-Hispanic group.

Suicide Method - Number of Suicide Deaths by Method

- Table 2 includes information on the total number of suicides for the most common methods.
- In 2014, firearms were the most common method used in suicide deaths in the United States, accounting for almost half of all suicide deaths (21,334).

Table 2. Suicide Method	Number of Deaths (2014)
Total	42,773
Firearm	21,334
Suffocation	11,407
Poisoning	6,808
Other	3,224

Data courtesy of CDC

Suicidal Thoughts and Behaviors Among U.S. Adults

- In Figure 7[1], data from the 2014 National Survey on Drug Use and Health (NSDUH) by the Substance Abuse and Mental Health Services Administration (SAMHSA) show that 3.9% of adults age 18 and older in the United States had thoughts about suicide in the past year.

- The percentage of adults having serious thoughts of suicide was highest among adults aged 18-25 (7.5%).

- The prevalence of suicidal thoughts was highest among adults reporting two or more races (8.3%).

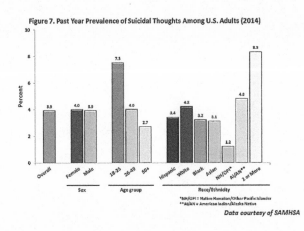

Figure 7. Past Year Prevalence of Suicidal Thoughts Among U.S. Adults (2014)

*NH/OPI = Native Hawaiian/Other Pacific Islander
**AI/AN = American Indian/Alaska Native

Data courtesy of SAMHSA

- Figure 8 [1] shows that in 2014, 9.4 million adults aged 18 or older reported having serious thoughts about trying to kill themselves, and 1.1 million adults aged 18 or older attempted suicide during the past year. Among those adults who attempted suicide, 0.9 million also reported making suicide plans.

Figure 8. Past Year Suicidal Thoughts and Behaviors Among U.S. Adults (2014)

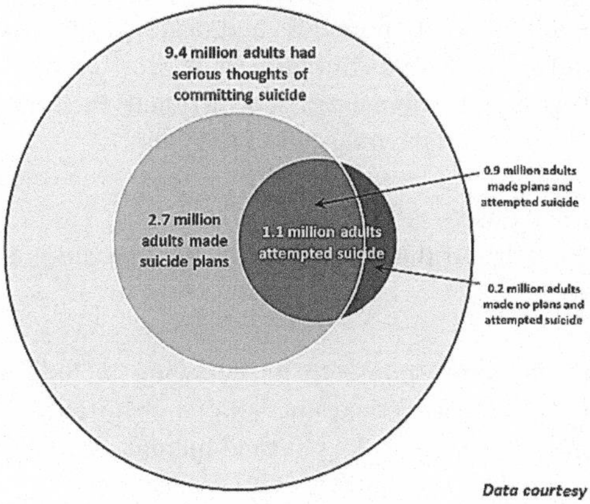

9.4 million adults had serious thoughts of committing suicide

2.7 million adults made suicide plans

1.1 million adults attempted suicide

0.9 million adults made plans and attempted suicide

0.2 million adults made no plans and attempted suicide

Data courtesy of SAMHSA

[1] **NSDUH Statistical Methods and Measurement**
Population:
• The survey participants are from a civilian, non-institutionalized population aged 18 years old or older residing within the United States. NSDUH does not ask adolescents aged 12 to 17 about suicidal thoughts and behavior.

• The survey covers residents of households (persons living in houses/townhouses, apartments, condominiums; civilians living in housing on military bases, etc.) and persons in non-institutional group quarters (e.g., shelters, rooming/boarding houses, college dormitories, migratory workers' camps, and halfway houses).

• The survey does not cover persons who, for the entire year, had no fixed address (e.g., homeless and/or transient persons not in shelters); were on active military duty; or who resided in institutional group quarters (e.g., correctional facilities, nursing homes, mental institutions, long-term hospitals).

Survey Non-response:
• In 2014, 29.7% of the NSDUH adult sample did not complete the interview.

• Reasons for non-response to interviewing include: refusal to participate (21.6%); respondent unavailable or no one at home/not answering the door (3.3%); physical/mental incompetence or language barriers (3.8%).

• People with suicidal behavior may disproportionately fall into these non-response categories. While NSDUH weighting includes non-response adjustments to reduce bias, these adjustments may not fully account for differential non-response by suicide behavior status.

• Please see the <u>2014 SAMHSA NSDUH Suicidal Thoughts and Behavior among Adults</u> report for further information on how these data were collected and calculated." (The National Institute of Mental Health (NIMH) is part of the National Institutes of Health (NIH), a component of the U.S. Department of Health and Human Services., n.d.)

Per publication (FS637) at North Dakota State University website:

"Youth and Suicide Trends

Because of the seriousness of the problem of suicide in the U.S., adults and youth should be aware of trends related to suicide and be prepared to discuss them. The following key points are important:

• Research suggests that **most adolescent suicides occur after school hours in the teen's home**, and often are related to some kind of interpersonal conflict with others.

• **Adolescent females are twice as likely as males to consider suicide seriously** (one in five to one in 10) or **attempt suicide** (one in 10 to one in 20), with Hispanic females being most likely to attempt suicide among female adolescents.

• **Adolescent males are much more likely to complete suicide than females**, averaging more than five times the suicide rate of similar-age females. From 1981 to 2013, more than 80 percent of 10- to 24-year-olds who committed suicide were male.

• **American Indian and Alaskan native male adolescents have the highest suicide rates**, with rates 1.5 to 3 times higher than that of similar-age males in other ethnic groups.

• **Firearms or suffocation were used** in over 80 percent of youth suicides in the last decade and typically are associated with lethal suicides, regardless of race or gender, accounting for more than four of five completed suicides.

• **Depression and a combination of aggressive behavior and/or substance abuse or anxiety** are found in more than half of all youth who commit suicide.

Key Points of Discussion Regarding Suicide

Parents and other adults are critical in helping children and youth understand and deal with issues related to suicide and suicidal ideation. Several key points may be useful in considering discussion regarding suicide:

• **Acknowledge the serious nature of suicide as a public health issue and both a personal and national tragedy**. Suicide should not be sensationalized and it should not be normalized when it is discussed. Approaching it from a straightforward and fact-based perspective that emphasizes causes and consequences is most helpful.

• **Directly and sensitively discuss suicide as a problem issue in a responsible way and help individuals process their feelings**. Approach the topic with the use of good information and available professional resources. Research has shown discussion of suicide with teens does not lead to any increased thinking about suicide or to suicidal behaviors. Responsible discussion can allow peers to identify others who may exhibit suicidal thinking or behaviors and give them support.

• **Identify clearly the factors that can make an individual more vulnerable to the risk of suicide**. The notion that a person who talks about suicide is unlikely to make an attempt at suicide is not true. Thoughts often lead to intentions and eventually to acts. Often a person who is vulnerable to the possibility of suicide does not have the emotional resources and support to cope with their challenges. Identifying and assisting individuals who are vulnerable is an important element of suicide prevention.

• **Take each person's feelings and actions regarding suicide seriously and assist individuals in getting support if needed**. Help children and youth realize that getting help from mental health professionals or other sources may be needed. Also, provide support, care and listening as needed to help individuals deal with personal challenges. Inform yourself and others about local and national resources you may access to assist someone." (Brotherson, 2016)

I continued my research and found more information regarding suicide deaths and suicide attempts. Per the American Foundation for Suicide Prevention website:

Suicide Statistics
"While this data is the most accurate we have, we estimate the numbers to be higher. Stigma surrounding suicide leads to underreporting, and data collection methods critical to suicide prevention need to be improved.

Suicide Attempts
No complete count is kept of suicide attempts in the U.S.; however, each year the CDC gathers data from hospitals on non-fatal injuries from self-harm.

494,169 people visited a hospital for injuries due to self-harm. This number suggests that approximately 12 people harm themselves for every reported death by suicide. However, because of the way these data are collected, we are not able to distinguish intentional suicide attempts from non-intentional self-harm behaviors.

Many suicide attempts, however, go unreported or untreated. Surveys suggest that at least one million people in the U.S. each year engage in intentionally inflicted self-harm.

Females attempt suicide three times more often than males. As with suicide deaths, rates of attempted suicide vary considerably among demographic groups. While males are 4 times more likely than females to die by suicide, females attempt suicide 3 times as often as males. The ratio of suicide attempts to suicide death in youth is estimated to be about 25:1, compared to about 4:1 in the elderly.

Per the American Foundation for Suicide Prevention website there were 44,193 suicide deaths in 2015, and an estimated 25 suicide attempts (1,104,825) for every suicide death." (American Foundation for Suicide Prevention, n.d.)

If we use the standard of 6 people being dramatically affected by a loved one's life and/or death, there are 6,628,950 people severely affected annually by a suicide attempt compared to 265,158 people grieving a suicide death.

2015 SUICIDE DEATHS, SUICIDE ATTEMPTS AND PEOPLE AFFECTED IN THE UNITED STATES

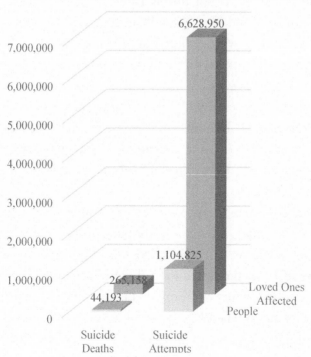

I was stunned.

How could this many people be affected by something and it remains widely ignored, terribly stigmatized, and continually dismissed?

I was confused! I was befuddled and astounded! I was horrified! I was outraged!

The anger that I had felt through my grieving process was magnified and the wounds torn open the more research I did. I was further hurt by the people and organizations I spoke with that continued to pacify me with the "call 1-800-273-TALK if I was in crisis" speech. I wanted to scream at them rather than continue to be professional. I wanted to throw statistics at them as proof that we needed to be validated and supported. We need help! We deserve resources! I am researching!

I contacted suicide prevention websites, suicide lifelines, suicide prevention organizations, mental health associations, therapists, doctors, and coalitions worldwide. I found out that indeed there was little or no help available for me "until my dad kills himself". I can only find support when I am a "suicide survivor". There was nothing for people who have someone they love attempt suicide. **Nothing.**

Am I the only one of these millions of people who wants resources? Am I the only one entrenched in grief? As I continued to do Internet searches regarding grief I learned there are a lot of different grief models. As I researched grief and thought about this book, and you the reader, I wondered, "Should I follow the Five Stages of Grief, the Seven Stages, or the Twelve Stages?"

Suicide attempts and grief are so complicated, and I want it simplified. Now, I realized loved ones of people who attempt suicide do experience disbelief and isolation; we absolutely got angry, and wanted to find acceptance. These are three of the five grief stages outlined at http://grief.com/the-five-stages-of-grief/. (Kessler, 2017) The Five Stages of Grief is simple widely known and accepted, and this is the model I chose.

You need to know I do understand the grief model I have chosen was created by the author specifically for people who are dying – Not for people who were diagnosed with cancer, who were fired, or who experienced the death of a loved one. Despite that fact, the model has been incorporated, accepted and widely used by different organizations, professionals and groups and is a model that is helpful for anyone working through grief or loss.

"Grief is not about clear, predictable stages or steps.

Rather, it is a natural process of dynamic changes that will ebb and flow as they may.

You experience grief across every dimension of your being – body, mind and spirit as author John Schneider says, Grief is a natural process of discovering what was lost, what is left, and what is possible.'" (Ellis, 2006)

Workbook

How does your loved one's suicide attempt
make you feel?

What do you wish the suicide attempter knew about your experience through this?

How do you feel about the attempter?

How does this feel like grief to you?

How does it feel different from other types of grief you have felt in the past?

What thoughts do you have you believe no one would understand if you said them aloud?

What are some things you did when you worked through other kinds of grief in your life?

Can you use those same tools now or do you need different ones?

A Suicide Attempt ~ The Five Stages of Grief or Loss for Loved Ones

Denial/Isolation
Anger
Bargaining/What If
Depression/Fear
Acceptance/Rebuilding

The stages of grief are not meant to tuck messy emotions into neat packages with a pretty bow on top. The five stages: denial/isolation, anger, bargaining, depression and acceptance are a part of the framework that makes up our learning to live with loss. They are tools to help us frame and identify what we may be feeling. They are not stops on a linear timeline in grief. Not everyone goes through all the stages, nor do people go through them in a prescribed order.

In fact, you may start in the depths of depression, move toward isolation, and then wake up somewhere in the bargaining stage. For people working through complicated grief some days these stages can be all meshed together like the colors on a child's finger-paint project and some months can be spent so smothered with anger you think you may never feel anything else ever again. They may be a lengthy cycle spent in something that may resemble a figure 8 pattern.

Because of this I wanted to know, "Is the grief work really necessary, or worth it?" Maybe I can continue to skip it all and take the advice of everyone who said, "What is the big deal? No one died." "Move on." "Get over it."

I asked Licensed Marriage and Family Therapist, Erik Cooper, what happens to people who have a loved one attempt suicide and are not allowed to grieve or don't work through their grief. He said, "They pretend like they have done the work. They put the subject way over here, out of their awareness so they don't have to look at it or deal with it. They change who they talk to. They change who they interact with. They change where they go and who they are. They change what shows they watch and what they listen to on the radio. They change because they believe it is easier than doing the work. They change so that the topic won't come up, so that the thorn that is right there doesn't get rubbed. That way they can pretend it doesn't matter." (Cooper, 2012)

Anna Adams, LPC gave this information, "When someone attempts suicide, everyone affected has a right to talk about it and name it. If we use different words like, 'accident', we blanket it and can't work through the trauma. When there is a suicide attempt there is trauma. Trauma for the person who attempted suicide and trauma for the family. If we use other words and phrases than 'suicide', it prevents rebuilding of trust in that relationship. The relationship will have an unhealthy dynamic and not naming it increases the likelihood of another attempt. The more transparent we are in our relationships the healthier we are and the healthier our relationships are." (Adams, 2017)

"To spare oneself from grief at all cost can be achieved only at the price of total detachment, which excludes the ability to experience happiness." Erich Fromm, Psychologist (Shantz Hertzler, 2017)

"If grief is refused a natural outlet, it chooses an unnatural and more destructive way to express itself.

The question is not whether or not you will mourn, but whether or not you allow yourself a constructive way to mourn.

And if you cut off natural outlets for mourning, the sadness will take its toll in other ways, sometimes on your body." (Rand, 1985)

Stage One ~ Denial and Isolation

We don't function well as human beings when we're in isolation.

Robert Zemeckis, Director & Producer

You're going through the horror of it, you're going through the isolation of it but you're being empowered by reminding yourself that you're connected to everybody else.

Adam Arkin, Actor

Grief can derange even the strongest and most disciplined of minds.

George R.R. Martin, Game of Thrones

One early reaction to learning about a loved one's suicide attempt is often denial. Denial provides shelter from the pain, confusion, endless questions, fear, shame, and possible anger. I don't think our minds are created to be able to comprehend an event such as a suicide attempt in one piece. Comprehension must be broken down into bite-sized bits. A lot of those bits are how this suicide attempt is simply not possible. As you work backwards from denial, you can create each bite sized bit you are denying into reality, slowly. Some very small little bits and pieces you can't comprehend may always be denied.

As David Kessler says, **"We wonder how we can go on, if we can go on, why we should go on. We try to find a way to simply get through each day. Denial and shock help us to cope and make survival possible. Denial helps us to pace our feelings of grief. There is a grace in denial. It is nature's way of letting in only as much as we can handle."** (Kubler-Ross, 2014)

The first stage of the grieving process regarding an attempted suicide is complete with isolation and disbelief. You may hear yourself saying, "No!" over and over again. You may deny that the attempt was an attempt. You may call it an accident. You may know it was an attempt but tell others it was an accident. You may deny that the event happened at all, or deny how it happened, or deny when it happened. You may deny what the attempt has done to your loved one's physical self – the physical damage, the mental damage, and the lasting effects of a mangled body or brain.

You may feel isolated after the suicide attempt because people won't talk about the subject or mention your loved one, who attempted. You may isolate yourself out of sheer exhaustion and inability to connect with anyone. You may isolate yourself because you were asked by the person who attempted to not tell anyone, meanwhile you can think of nothing else but the attempt. You may isolate yourself, hiding in your guilt, anger, shame or embarrassment. Finding others who have had this experience and learning from them was difficult for me. Isolation and denial are close companions when dealing with a suicide attempt.

"The problem with suffering in silence is that you don't have support when you need it most." Mary McCambridge, grief counselor and founder of the Foundation for Grieving Children
(Vatner, 2009)

"When you're in mourning, it's easy to feel that nobody understands what you're going through. And this is particularly true with 'disenfranchised grief.'" Kenneth J. Dako, PhD, Professor of Gerontology at the College of New Rochelle in New York (Vatner, 2009)

What Can I Do?

1. **Recognize and accept there is nothing wrong with you.** Whatever your feelings are, they are legitimate. You don't need anyone to tell you that you can think or feel what you are thinking and feeling. Just experience it. Let the feelings pass through you like you are a screen. If you try to deny or fight the thoughts or feelings, they will become blocked up inside of you and you will eventually need to release them to become healthy. Remember that denial is one of the tools of healing. Use it as a tool to heal, not commit more damage.

2. **Find people who will understand** if you are willing and able. This may take work you may not be willing to do right away but when you are ready:
   - **Ask for support** in your faith/spiritual group or from your friends.
   - **Conduct an online search** AttemptedSuicideHelp.com has resources and excerpts of others stories dealing with attempted suicide.
   - **Find a support "group"** While there may not be support groups for this kind of grief there may be other support systems you find. Research indicates people seeking a support regarding attempted suicide will not actually go

to a support group for family and friends of suicide attempters. Support groups have been formed across the nation for this population with no attendance. This leads me to encourage you to find support systems, cooking classes, exercise groups, a faith group, or bible study. The more systems or groups you have to rely on the better. The power of these groups is that they are not focused on your grief but on something else that will allow you to feel connected and supported in life.

- **Let close friends know you are looking for support.** They may be able to find tools, grief coaches or counselors, other resources, or offer more support for you when they know you are open to support and actively looking.

3. **Be honest about how you feel.** If a well-meaning friend cracks a joke about your loved one or the suicide attempt, explain that this experience is painful for you.

4. **Develop a ritual or ceremony to commemorate your loss.** Take as much time as you need to express your feelings of grief and pain. Rituals are powerful and we have relied on them as human beings for as long as we have existed. Talk to the four winds, write your experience on paper and then burn it, meditate at the same spot, create art, do something that speaks to you and continue to do it

over and over until you feel better. This is not a onetime thing.

5. **Take care of yourself.** Rest and sleep when you need it. Drink plenty of water and get fresh air, sunshine and exercise. I realize looking back, the things that made this hardest on me is how hard I was on myself because of what people had said to me. I just kept thinking I should be way better than I was and feel so much more healthy and happy than I did because people said I should. And so, I pressed on and didn't allow me to take care of me because I was told there should be nothing wrong with me. I am allowing and encouraging you to be honest with you and to take great care of you.

6. **Find a therapist.** I did not do this and wish I would have. I didn't because I was afraid of the cost. I was helping my children work through their emotions and thoughts, and I hadn't found anything helpful. Thus, I was afraid I would find a therapist who reiterated I had no right to feel what I was feeling. What I realize now is that I probably would have only needed to go for a few months and would have gained a lot of tools. I may not have found a great therapist right away, but I would have been a lot healthier a lot quicker if I would have looked and worked to find professional help. Your grief process is not a forever sentence, but it is something you

may need professional help to work through and get beyond.

7. **Talk about it.** Find as many people as you can that you trust and just talk it through. I only had one friend that could hear what I had to say through this whole experience. She would not judge or make suggestions but just loved me through it all. I wish I would have had more friends like her, but one friend was amazing and our friendship survived and is thriving because she could just be with me through the pain. I think hearing your own voice say something out loud, where another human being can hear what you say is a very powerful very therapeutic event that is very necessary. This is one essential thing you can do to work through the denial and the isolation. Hearing your voice say something makes the event more tangible and saying it to a trusted loving human bridges the gap of isolation.

"If we don't take care of ourselves or allow ourselves to grieve, some of the physical problems that might arise include sleeplessness, heart palpitations, irregular breathing, gastrointestinal difficulties, a choking sensation, weight loss, shingles, and chronic illness.

That's just the top of the list. If we don't forge down the grief path, these difficulties will come back at least two-fold one day when our bodies can't bear the grief any longer...

In basic terms, it's essential we take good care of ourselves and give ourselves time to heal." (Linn-Gust, 2007)

Workbook

Who are three people I trust and feel comfortable sharing my thoughts and feelings with about the suicide attempt?

What are four of my favorite ways to take care of or pamper myself?

What are five things I can do to work through my denial and possible isolation and who can help me with this?

Who are three professional therapists or grief specialists I can get appointments with including their name and contact information?

Do I need to have a main contact person who communicates updates of well-being and needs with my friends and family? Who are the people that could be? Include their contact information:

Notable Quotes

These quotes highlight a sample of how people felt after the suicide attempt. They show the denial and isolation interviewees felt at some point during their grieving process. The challenges are many.

1) Family and friends simply do not know how to address the suicide attempt.

2)The person dealing with the suicide attempt of a loved one does not know how to address the suicide attempt with his or her support network to help the network provide the support needed.

3) Many of us may be isolating ourselves either out of fear or guilt, or out of pain from the reactions we have received from family, friends, and society.

"You find you have a hard time getting help from within [your own] family to deal with a lot of this. A meteor came and crashed in our life. We couldn't recognize any of the landscape. Our extended family was nowhere to be found. They are still unavailable to this day."

"The horror of the physical wounds was scary, horrible to look at. The inability to share with people who could support me made me feel alone and helpless."

"I found the sibling survivor network, but I posted something and got the typical response: 'would trade places with you in a heartbeat.' I did not find what I was looking for, not at all. I found quite the opposite. I found guilt-inducing people who made me feel like I was ungrateful because my brother is alive."

"I was very upset and isolated by the fact that none of my family members (grandparents, aunts, uncles and cousins) have expressed any concern, care, remorse, support or thoughts, even to this day. The in-laws that ask about my family purposely exclude asking about my dad now. I don't know if it is because they don't want to know, don't care, or don't want to bring up the subject. I was most surprised by the number of relationships and people I lost. It has been a very long, lonely, violating, sorrowful process."

"The lack of support from any of my extended family was so painful and isolating. Not one aunt, uncle, cousin or grandparent called or checked on me. I thought we used to be a close family. To have the attempt and then lose the support of a family you thought you had is devastating."

"My friends couldn't understand the full impact of the situation. They didn't understand the emotional impact of potentially losing someone you love and not being able to help them."

"There are probably times when I don't bring up my personal experience with attempted suicide because I don't feel people have the ability to understand. There is a lot of fear in me that people will run away from it."

"I called everywhere for help. The leader for a local support group for suicide survivors told me he would give anything to have his son back, even for a day. He said I didn't understand suicide. He told me because of the nature of the suicide attempts my loved one would eventually kill himself, and when he did I was welcome to join their group. Until then he had no resources or help for me."

"The trickledown effect is horrific. This affects everything and everyone in my life."

"The weeping often endures for such a long, long night that we tend to wonder if we'll ever feel familiar with ourselves again.

Feel relief again. Feel free to hum a little tune again.

Will the time ever come when we can be greeted at the grocery store of on the street – freely, without embarrassment for our friends?

Without their having to wonder because of some look in our eyes, just what to say in the face of such long lasting grief." (Price, 1983)

Stage Two ~ Anger

Anger as soon as fed is dead-'Tis starving makes it fat.

Emily Dickinson, Poet

Do not teach your children never to be angry; teach them how to be angry.

Lyman Abbott, Author

Usually when people are sad, they don't do anything. They just cry over their condition. But when they get angry, they bring about a change.

James Russell Lowell, Poet

Suppressed grief suffocates, it rages within the breast, and is forced to multiply its strength.

Ovid, Poet

A nger is necessary but also very scary for most people. The anger that comes with an attempted suicide is terrifying. Anger may come in waves or may set up camp and be the only thing you feel. You may work so hard to deny your anger that you become exhausted. Anger is such a strong emotion that you may fight against it. You want to be fine. You want to move on. You may find if you welcome anger that you get to a point that you don't want to feel angry anymore, and yet the anger remains. Everyone's experience with anger can be different.

David Kessler says, **"Anger is a necessary stage of the healing process. Be willing to feel your anger, even though it may seem endless. The more you truly feel it, the more it will begin to dissipate and the more you will heal. There are many other emotions under the anger and you will get to them in time, but anger is the emotion we are most used to managing. The truth is that anger has no limits. It can extend not only to your friends, the doctors, your family, yourself and your loved one... but also to God. You may ask, 'Where is God in this?' Underneath anger is pain, your pain. It is natural to feel deserted and abandoned, but we live in a society that fears anger. Anger is strength and it can be an anchor, giving temporary structure...We usually know more about suppressing anger than feeling it. The anger is just**

another indication of the intensity of your love."
(Kessler, 2017)

I am an advocate for anger. Anger helped me – I like anger -- the energy behind it, the passion and the fact that it can be a catalyst to getting better, getting healthy, and being well.

One of the ways I dealt with my anger was to go trail running. Reflecting on my experience, I still can't believe I did that. I am not a runner. I hate running. But when faced with the burst of energy and burning tears my anger provided, there was nothing else I could do but run until my legs ached, my lungs nearly burst, and my feet were on fire. I only ran for a few months. Now I feel no desire to ever run again, and yet I can remember the feeling of needing to run more than I needed air in my lungs.

There are a lot of different online tools, therapies, books, work books, and support groups for anger and anger management you can seek out and use. Or you can hire a professional therapist who specializes in grief or anger if you feel you are stuck and can't move on.

Leland R. Beaumont via the website emotionalcompetency.com shares the "Benefits and Dangers of Anger. The anger mechanism would not have survived millions of years of evolution if it did not provide important survival benefits.

Here are some of those benefits:
- Anger tells us that something needs to change.
- Anger can provide the motivation to constructively change whatever it was that caused the anger. It can energize the fight for legitimate rights. It contributed to eliminating slavery and apartheid, and lead to women's suffrage and civil rights. Anger can motivate us to overcome oppression and topple a tyrant.
- Anger can provide the motivation to constructively correct an injustice. It urges us to act on our sense of justice.
- Anger can provide the motivation to constructively teach offenders what they did to make you angry, and to learn to act differently.
- Anger can help to reduce or overcome fear and provide the energy needed to mobilize needed change.
- Anger sends a powerful signal that informs others of trouble. It notifies the offender that you have perceived an offense.
- Anger helps us to preserve our ego and think good of ourselves.
- Anger is a normal response to an external stimulus that needs to be addressed.

One of the most dangerous features of anger is that expressing anger increases the anger of others. This can lead to a rapid and dangerous escalation. We may try to harm the target of our anger. We often wish them harm. The impulse to harm is probably a central part of the anger response for most people. While anger can be dangerous and must be constrained, it cannot and should not be eliminated." (Beaumont, 2009)

You may be angry after a suicide attempt because you feel you weren't enough for the person who attempted to live for. Some of your anger may come from the fact that you feel you are owed an explanation, or an apology, and never received either. You may be angry at yourself or others for not knowing the attempt was coming. All those feelings are valid; however, no matter what the attempter says, the suicide attempt is not about you.

In retrospect, I was most angry that everything I found drove home that people never recover after a suicide death. They are never the same. They are devastated, tortured, and affected every minute of every day of their life. That made me so terribly angry because I didn't want to believe that. I didn't want my life to be a disaster zone. That is not what I signed up for and it is not what I wanted for my children.

That anger drove me to find out if my life could indeed be rebuilt. It led me to seek people who can, and did, heal their lives and were now healthy after loss. I know now that I don't think of suicide and suicide attempts every day, but I did for years. I know now that I can be healthy and happy and have healthy, supportive, happy relationships. I had to feel my anger, and use it, to come to that realization.

"The most common emotion I have seen after a suicide attempt, for family members, is anger and then blame. Self-blame and blaming the person who attempted suicide." (Adams, 2017)

What Can I Do?

1. **Find a physical outlet for your anger.** This can be something you have done your whole life. One person I interviewed played tennis three to four times a week because she could be with people she had known for years and not have to talk. It could be something like me running, which I didn't do before and may never do again. This may take trial and error. You may take a free Karate class or dance class to see if it works for you. You may just start walking and know that is enough. You may buy a punching bag and some gloves. You may start Yoga and find your center. Find a physical outlet for your anger.

2. **Write.** Write a Blog or write in a journal or a notebook. Write your feelings, your anger, your fears, and your thoughts. I was not able to write for two years after my dad's second attempt. I used to write in journals or notebooks all the time. I would write my experiences or write poems. I loved to write. However, after the attempts I simply could not write. I would sit with a pen in my hand over paper and have so many words going through my head and I couldn't write a damn thing. Then one day the words demanded that I sit down for a long time and write and write and write. So, write if you

can. Journaling is very helpful for many people in their anger phase and a step toward healing. Writing for me now has been instrumental and an irreplaceable tool for my healing and releasing.

3. **Give yourself permission to feel your anger.** If you are spending a lot of your time and energy denying your anger or telling yourself you don't have a reason to feel angry, you are not living in the moment. Work through that anger. Don't feel strange if you haven't felt anger yet. If you are working through the grieving process the anger may eventually show up and when it does you will know it, and at that time, give yourself permission to feel it.

4. **Meditate.** Turn off all electronic devices so you will not be distracted. I cannot sit and textbook meditate for more than about 5 minutes, but that is where I start, and restart and restart. I found that by turning off my radio, cell phone, house phone, television, and computer my brain knew it would not be interrupted in its process. So, while I can only sit in a cross legged position for about 5 minutes my body, heart, and soul know that they have 30 minutes to work through whatever comes up without interruption because that is how long I give it. I recommend at least 30 minutes of time daily because the frantic pace created by a suicide

attempt crisis makes this ritual a necessity for your health. There are meditation apps for smart phones that set your phone to airplane mode for a set amount of time. There are also a lot of books or classes you can take through recreation districts or your library you may find helpful. All these are tools to help you find a meditation practice that works best for your mind, body, and soul. If you choose to not call it meditation that is great. Just make sure to take at least 30 minutes a day of uninterrupted quiet for you.

5. **Hire a professional.** This can be your therapist who gives you more tools to use on your own. It can be a professional mediator to work through this anger with you and the suicide attempter. It could be a personal trainer. It could be an art teacher. It could be all. There are people who are trained and educated to help you with many things, including anger. Utilize these professionals. Again, this is not a life sentence. It is not the whole book of your life. It is a page, or a chapter in the story. Hire a professional and gain the tools you need.

6. **Set healthy boundaries.** This was a very difficult step for me because I couldn't figure out what was healthy. I was so damaged that everything, every thought, felt terrible. Any boundary I tried to set felt like I was victimizing my family members or

isolating myself further. This step took me years to figure out. The boundaries you and your loved one set may change. Just because one week you say you will only speak about the suicide attempt for 10 minutes each phone conversation, doesn't mean that is set in stone for the rest of your life. Be clear with others that your boundaries can change and that others can change their boundaries also. Be aware when boundaries have been nonexistent in a relationship it is common for someone to set a very strict far-fetched boundary trying to find some balance.

This is all a part of learning to set healthy boundaries. Be patient with yourself and others and continue to work together. Don't get lost in the thinking that because it is a work in progress that the work isn't important. You are bringing hurt people together to a damaged relationship working to make the people and the relationship healthy. This will be a work in progress for some time.

"Don't bottle up shame or guilt.
Schedule regular times for
unburdening with a spiritual advisor,
counselor, or therapist or trusted
friend."

Oprah Winfrey, Media Proprietor

<u>Workbook</u>

What are four physical things I can do when feeling angry to relieve some of my emotions?

What time of day will work best for me to unplug and meditate? Schedule that time in your calendar each day.

What are ways I have seen others deal with their anger? Are these ways physically and emotionally healthy?

Would any of the healthy ways work for me?
Which ones?

What are four boundaries I see I need to set in my life or relationships to create health, accountability and balance?

What are three additional healthy ways to deal with my anger? List them here:

What can feeling my anger help me do?

Notable Quotes

*If I had to pick one word that universally described loved ones after a suicide attempt, during some point in their recovery, I would pick **angry**. Most are angry at the attempter, angry at themselves, angry at their friends and family, and even angry at God. Many of these quotes are difficult to read. It is anger in its purest sense. The second word I would pick to describe the emotion that surfaces again and again is guilt. Guilt for not knowing this was coming. Guilt for not doing something or not being able to change this trajectory. Guilt for feeling so angry.*

"I was learning to be detached. There were moments of anger, resentment, doubt, and self-doubt."

"I had a lot of guilt. I felt like it was somehow my fault the attempt had happened. I was helpless, angry, and experienced all the normal feelings surrounding any type of loss. I guess most people think I didn't lose anything, but there was an extreme sense of loss anyway."

"I was surprised by the anger I felt when the physical wounds from the attempt healed."

"I was surprised at the fact I wanted him dead. I wished he had succeeded in killing himself."

"I got so angry I thought I was going to pass out. I was seething with anger. I have never been that angry in my life."

Stage Three ~ Bargaining and What If?

You can spend twenty-four hours a day feeling your loved one's pain for them. You can put your life on hold, waiting for them to come around to your way of thinking. You can let your entire emotional life be dictated by their mood of the moment. But none of that will help...

(Mason & Kreger, 1998)

The question is not why or how but what? What is happening and what is the next action that can be taken...Who do we help by getting stuck in the why's and how's? We help no one.

(Tallard Johnson, 1988)

Bargaining may be a small step, a large step, or a convoluted step in your grief process. You may have done all your bargaining before the attempt. You may have prayed to God. Questioned the therapist. Pleaded with the attempter. Asked for healing. Begged the attempter to take medication as prescribed, to attend their appointment, to think different thoughts, act different ways, and say different things.

You may feel blindsided by the suicide attempt because you thought everything was getting better. You may ask "Why?" "Why" is a part of the bargaining stage. You think that if you know why this attempt happened then you can fix the problem. You think you can make it not ever happen to anyone ever again.

Bargaining includes the "What ifs", "If Onlys", "How could it be different?" and "What could I have done?" What you really are looking for is your life to return to the way it was before the attempt. You want your own normal back. You also want a guarantee that this will never happen again, to you, or anyone you love.

David Kessler states, **"Guilt is often bargaining's companion. The 'if onlys' cause us to find fault in ourselves and what we "think" we could have done differently. We may even bargain with the pain. We will do anything not to feel the_____. We remain in**

91

the past, trying to negotiate our way out of the hurt.
People often think of the stages as lasting weeks or
months. They forget that the stages are responses to
feelings that can last for minutes or hours as we flip
in and out of one and then another. We do not enter
and leave each individual stage in a linear fashion.
We may feel one, then another and back again to the
first one." (Kessler, 2017)

How many of us have ever looked back on our lives
and said, "I wish I had known then what I know now?"
Most of us have said this, but we were looking at our
high school years, parenting challenges, and other
"normal" life events. We never dreamed we would be
asking this question after a catastrophic suicide attempt.
But we have joined this club now, and many of us are
saying, "I wish I had known…." Bargaining and saying,
"What if?" are normal stages of the grieving process
and normal reactions to an attempted suicide.

Loved ones I interviewed spent hours at the beginning
stages of their healing process reading, researching, and
suggesting things to help the attempter recover, "get
better," and live a healthy, "normal" life. They created
situations where the attempter did not have to face
normal consequences for their attempt and other
behaviors and choices.

Additionally, these people ended up spending their time, money, and energy, often jeopardizing their own lives, trying to help the attempter, while neglecting their personal physical, mental, emotional and spiritual health. They hoped once they "fixed" the attempter's problems, things would suddenly be back to normal in their lives and the possibility of life being normal again would be likely.

"What I realized in my grief work, is that everything really did have its place.

Everything – all the pain and the suffering - really did have its' meaning.

I didn't have to be the one to figure it out though. That wasn't my work.

My job was to be with it...to embrace it fully. Eventually I stopped asking, 'Why my son?' 'Why me?' because the flip side to that is, 'Why not?' 'Why not me?'

Maybe the thing about people seeking and needing closure is that they are still asking the question, 'Why?'"
(Blowey, 2013)

"The bargaining stage may occur prior to loss as well as after loss, as an attempt to negotiate pain away. The

bargaining stage is characterized by attempting to negotiate with a higher power or someone or something you feel, whether realistically or not, that has some control over the situation. You may make promises to God in return for the painful situation not to occur or for things to go back to how they were before the loss or change, according to Kübler-Ross and David Kessler.

In the bargaining stage, you may find yourself intensely focused on what you or others could have done differently in order to prevent the loss or change. You may also think about all the things that could have been and how wonderful life would have been if not for this unpleasant situation. While these thoughts may help you begin to accept the loss or change by revealing the impact of the situation, North Carolina A&T State University warns that these feelings can also lead to remorse and guilt that interfere with healing.

Prevention - *MedlinePlus notes that grief is a healthy process and should not be prevented. As a part of the grieving process, the bargaining stage should therefore not be prevented. Watching someone you love experience the bargaining stage, and grief in general, may be difficult, but respecting the process is essential to the eventual acceptance of loss and change.*

Time Frame - No set time frame for experiencing grief exists, nor does the bargaining stage require a certain length of time to process. Each individual is unique, and each individual will require different lengths of time for each stage and for the process as a whole. In fact, you do not need to experience all of the stages to heal. You may skip the bargaining stage, or all of the stages of grief, and still find acceptance and resolution. Helpguide.org further explains that if you do experience the stages of grief as outlined by Kübler-Ross, you may experience them out of order." (Aiger, 2015)

All this information supported what I, and others I interviewed, experienced. We wanted to be responsible for the suicide attempt in some way so we could make it not happen again. We also didn't want to be responsible what so ever, but were afraid of not being accountable; because, as humans, we want to be able to control the outcome. We do want ownership in our life and the result. We want to know we matter and can make a difference. We also know in our hearts that the choices others make in their lives are not our responsibility.

All of this is the bargaining stage. The truth is you do make a difference. And you are not the only piece of the puzzle. You get to decide how your piece of the puzzle looks, acts, and feels to yourself and others. That is all you can control.

"I think it is important for family members of someone who has attempted suicide to know they can feel <u>empowered AND powerless</u> at the same time.

They can feel empowered when they know what they can manage. They are empowered when they are advocating for their self and their loved one.

They feel powerless knowing they don't get to make the decisions.

Knowing they can feel both at the same time is important." (Adams, 2017)

"I think, because we assume that the

depth of our love is a testament to our caring, we assume that it should also be enough to fix the attempter and the problem.

Obviously, that is not the case.

We all think we have so much responsibility for someone else's life.

We are responsible for our actions and how it affects someone but we can't fix them or make them do something they don't really want to do." (Blowey, 2013)

What Can I Do?

1. **List ways in which you bargained with the attempter before the attempt, if applicable.** This is a way you can reflect on your actions and see what was effective and what may have been futile. Frequently after a suicide attempt the attempter blames those closest to them and lashes out. If this has happened to you, this step will allow you to see what actions you did take and ways you thought you were helping.

2. **What are some ways you have been bargaining now? Who have you been bargaining with?** By using the word bargaining rather than the words helping, controlling, assisting, or doing, it allows you to step out from the caregiver or caretaker roll and see the situation with a new perspective or different eyes.

3. **What is one way you can take back power by asking the question, "What can I do now?"** By asking, "What can I do now?" you get back the power to create action or an action plan. It will give you the freedom to step out from the victim role.

100

<u>Workbook</u>

What have I learned since the attempt about the attempter and the action to end his/her life?

What would I do differently knowing what I have learned?

Do you believe this would have really made a difference in the short term/long-term?

What can you do now? One giant step away from the bargaining stage and the question "Why?" are action questions; What can I do now?

How can I help?

What can be changed?

What am I doing?

What am I feeling?

What do I want to do?

What am I afraid of?

What will I do if what I am afraid of happens?

Is there anything I can do to prevent it from happening?

Can I get support to prevent my fear from happening?

If my best friend told me he/she was afraid of the same thing what advice would I offer?

Notable Quotes

It would be great if we all lived a life without regrets. Unfortunately, we don't. When dealing with an attempted suicide, you may find you are full of regrets you would never have considered before. Here are a few of the things interviewees regretted...or didn't regret...and a glimpse into their bargaining stage of the grief process.

"Whether you lose someone or not you still have the same feelings of not being able to change the situation. It is a helpless feeling. You are watching it all unfold without the ability to change anything, no matter what your actions are."

"I was shocked it had built up behind my back or below the level of my awareness. I was surprised I could be so out of touch with the needs and reality of my own child."

"I wish I would have known early on that just listening and staying detached would have solved a lot of problems. I was always trying to convince him [the attempter] he was good enough and tried to validate him. But he only wanted me to listen to him."

"I wish I would have been more aware of my daughter's sickness because of her history of trauma. I wish I would have known my family and I were not alone in their experience."

"I wish I would have known I did not have the control over someone else that I thought I did. A lot of my frustration came from thinking we could lay out a treatment plan and everyone would comply."

"I regret I didn't have a closer relationship with my brother."

"I regret letting things get to that point. I still believe I had some control over the attempter."

"I guess the biggest thing is making sure I distance myself from the situation. I remind myself it is not my fault."

"Before I came to the realization I couldn't fix him I was having a hard time sleeping. I was consumed, almost obsessed, thinking about it. I wanted to find a solution, make a plan, fix what we could fix, and do what we can do. I suppose it was just the continuing search for answers and education that led me to the right answer. I cannot fix this."

"I regret pushing him away emotionally out of fear that the final suicide attempt would be too hard to live with and I would end up unable to function mentally and emotionally."

"The night before the suicide attempt, I regret I didn't ask more direct questions. Sometimes it feels like things and anger are being directed at me but there are issues beyond me I can't see. I wish I had better tools, training and ideas of what to do in a suicidal situation. Next time I will ask more direct questions. It is better than the worst alternative and better than dealing with a hospitalization, insurance, and a physically and emotionally damaged person whom I love."

"I don't think I regret anything other than the events leading up to how the suicide attempt happened. I think I probably would have been a little more sympathetic and tried to defuse the situations. I would like to believe if I had it to do over again I would not let it get to that point. I don't know if that would have changed anything but there are things I look at and say, 'If I would have pushed things and been more adamant about things like treatment…' But, you don't know for sure. You don't know if it really would change anything or made it so a suicide attempt wouldn't have happened. Maybe it would have pushed things and the attempter would complete. I don't know if you can necessarily fully change a suicidal situation."

"The key issue in grief is not to assess what types of losses are easier or harder, but rather to review factors that complicate, or facilitate, loss in each different circumstance."

(Hospice Foundation of America, 1997)

Stage Four ~ Depression and Fear

If grief is a process of healing, then depression is one of the many necessary steps along the way.

Elisabeth Kübler Ross, Psychiatrist

Confront your fears, list them, get to know them, and only then will you be able to put them aside and move ahead.

Jerry Gille

For me, depression was the direct result of trying so hard to be "normal" and not be angry. It exhausted me. I fought for two years to look fine, to carry on, to put on my big girl panties, cowgirl up, and pull myself up by my boot straps. I didn't want the suicide attempt to affect me. I wanted to be stronger, better, and be able to carry on. I desperately wanted better for my life and for my kid's lives.

"After bargaining, our attention moves squarely into the present. Empty feelings present themselves, and grief enters our lives on a deeper level, deeper than we ever imagined. This depressive stage feels as though it will last forever. It's important to understand that this depression (may or may not be) a sign of mental illness. It is the appropriate response to a great loss. We withdraw from life, left in a fog of intense sadness, wondering, perhaps, if there is any point in going on alone. Why go on at all? Depression after a loss is too often seen as unnatural: a state to be fixed, something to snap out of. The first question to ask yourself is whether or not the situation you're in is actually depressing." (Kessler, 2017)

One thing I learned in this process is that I love to replace the word "normal" with the word "healthy." I would say things like, "I just want to be normal." Or, "What is the normal way to handle this?" Listen folks, normal may not be good. The way everyone else normally handles things may work for them and may not work for you. So, now I want to be healthy. I want to handle things in a healthy way. I now say thing like, "I just want to be healthy," and, "What is the healthy way to handle this?"

I also believe, from my interviews and own experiences, the emotions and thoughts that cause people to attempt to end their lives get spread like a virus all over their loved ones during the suicide attempt. All the depression, anger, rage, hurt, isolation, fear, and belief of being unworthy and not belonging, that someone carries before an attempt is shared like an infection upon hearing of the attempt.

Healthy people in a family are now visibly not healthy or well at all. Individuals who were balanced and thriving prior to the suicide attempt of a loved one are now not able to get out of bed. It may not be to this extent in your family but there may be some signs of unrest and illness in everyone now. These signs may not have been there prior to the attempt. Schedule appointments and visit a therapist to talk about your own depression, fears, and thoughts of suicide that may have surfaced in you since the attempt.

A suicide attempt is depressing. It is heart wrenching to learn that someone you love dearly is in so much pain

124

they can no longer bear the thought of living. Experiencing depression after a loved one's suicide attempt is a normal and appropriate response. You want to hide. You may feel embarrassed, guilty, responsible, and fearful of another attempt or an attempt from someone else near to you. I think if you do not experience some depression after this event it would be unusual.

Some effects people reported after a loved one's suicide attempt include a complete inability to concentrate. Others feel like they have blacked out for months at a time with no recollection of events that occurred. Some suffer a sense of blurry or fuzzy emotions with no concrete memories. Many said they were present physically but not mentally or emotionally. For some, years were lost to the grief and despair while they were working through this process.

I tried so hard to remain a loving wife and parent that even though I cried for up to eight hours every day for two years, I buried a lot of my own fear and anger. I didn't want to feel depressed because I had a good life that included a healthy marriage and children. I didn't give myself permission to feel what I was feeling. I wanted this experience to have never happened and I assumed the next best thing was just acting like it hadn't. I didn't know how I was going to find closure, or an ending to my pain, <u>ever.</u>

I've since learned that most
psychologists define depression as
anger turned inward.

At that point in my experience being
angry with God was absolutely not
acceptable.

Being guilty and depressed were.

So subconsciously I had chosen what I
felt was the lesser of the two cosmic
evils." (Rand, 1985)

What I understand now is, "After a suicide attempt the family unit is fractured. I understand the challenge to (finding help) is the difficulty in finding a counselor or therapist who is going to walk that walk with you. Do your research. It is much easier to be handed the magic pill but you must empower yourself and do the work. I think most people who live through loving someone who attempted suicide want to have resolution, reconciliation and understanding while longing for, and calling it closure. What people need to understand about grief is that there isn't ever going to be closure. It isn't about closure. It is about integrating the experience and the pain, and living *with it* on various levels. It is a lifelong process. Grief changes for everyone and it evolves. It changes with new perspective. It changes with new experiences and understanding. It also brings up new questions. The work is never done." (Blowey, 2013)

Because I didn't understand my life could be whole and healthy while working through, living with and integrating this experience into my life I suppressed everything about it I could. That suppression led to a major breakdown after two years. This is one of my journal entries from that time:

I feel very sad, angry and alone. Every time I think that things are getting better and I am healing and moving on, there comes a day that I can't stop crying, don't want to get out of bed, parent my children, clean the house, be a wife or do anything. I am finding it hard on these occasions to have any hope for the future. I am so fortunate in all that I have. It is hard to explain to people how I feel or why I feel that way.

Some days I want to surround myself with people and chat about meaningless things. Most days I would rather talk about me and all the pain that I have been through and don't seem to move past. Other days I couldn't care less if I ever saw another living person again. On those days, it seems that everything others do makes me so angry and upset. From persons driving like idiots in traffic to mean, rude people in a store. It seems to just set me off and make me feel so resentful that people can get away with treating others in that manner. It makes me angry that I don't act that way and seem to be the person whom always gets annihilated emotionally, financially etc.

My kids are fabulous and I don't want to deal with them. My husband is the greatest thing in the world and I don't want to connect, communicate, open up or be intimate with him. I suppose I feel like I am not taken care of and feel completely unable to be responsible for anyone else at any time. I seem to do better one-on-one but fall apart when there are a lot of responsibilities or people, or things that I must do or accomplish. I have never been an angry person and find myself being set off by the most ridiculous circumstances or events. I feel as though I have dragged myself through the last two years unsuccessfully and almost dread every day or moment that comes. I don't know if I need a very serious break or what. I didn't have my children yesterday and I almost found myself worse off, which is surprising.

I feel so misunderstood and alone. I am surprised at the number of tears that I can cry and not run out. I am surprised at the number of people who have simply dropped out of my life and have no concern about me, or my wellbeing. These are friends and family I used to think were good people.

I deserve so much better than this and at the same time I have it so good. It is like I can see what I do have and how that should make me feel in my life but I am so empty and devoid of any emotion but fear, pain, anger and sadness that I can't drag my heart to where my body is. Strange. I am not sure but it is almost more hurtful when people assume that I should not feel this way and then I feel like I am either crazy or trying to justify my mental and emotional state.

Why can't I be completely wrecked about my dad shooting himself? Why can't I be an alcoholic mess? Why should I want to get out of bed, put on a happy face and greet the day?

I know this is affecting my kids and I hate that and resent it but can't seem to do anything to change it. I try to spend time with them, listen to them, hug them, love them, respect them and honor them and it doesn't seem to be enough.

I know they can sense that I am not right and maybe that is why. I just don't know how to get it right. I don't know how to pull myself together. I don't know how to move on or move past this.

I am so completely blown away by all the ways this event has affected and changed my life and myself. I wish I could make it all go away and get back to good.

Get back to the place where I could fool myself into thinking people actually cared about me. Get back to the place where I could laugh about something normal without having a drink in my belly. Get back to the place where jokes about head wounds and sure shots weren't the only thing that would make me giggle without a drink. Back to the place where black humor wasn't the only humor I know."

As you can see anger and depression were running rampant in me. Shortly after this entry I had a major break down and had to get help. I am forever grateful to my OB/GYN doctor for being willing to see me and prescribe medication that had worked for me before when I had experienced a prior life changing event. It took me all day wearing sun glasses and sobbing hysterically, several different waiting rooms at county buildings, therapists' offices, and mental health facilities. They all turned me away because I couldn't pay that day, or I didn't have insurance, or they didn't have an appointment for 11 weeks, but, "Hang in there. It isn't as bad as you think it is."

Frustrated and deflated and having only one other option I sat in my car that afternoon and called my OB/GYN office sobbing and shared what I had been through that day (they knew of my father's suicide attempts). His receptionist transferred me directly to him. He told me to come right in, even though I had no ability to pay for an office visit or medicine at that time. He gave me enough samples for a couple of months, called and checked on me several times to make sure the medication was working properly and I didn't have any adverse side effects, and told me to come back in a couple of months and he would give me more. He was an answer I needed. He knew the crisis I was in and one tool I needed I couldn't provide myself.

I chose to share this story with you because I want you to know to not give up. It isn't easy. It seems hopeless and ridiculous what you may have to endure to get help.

When you know you are in the throes of depression and need help, do not stop until you get it. Do not stop until someone hears you. Advocate for your crazy depressed sobbing nonsensical self. You are valuable and worth it.

"If people aren't afraid to talk about suicide, or a suicide attempt, it helps everyone.

There are a lot of places people can find support including counseling, churches, community groups, family and friends.

Counseling is just one piece of that network that can be important depending on the family dynamic and individual. Some family relationships absolutely need professional help, and for some family relationships have strong natural support networks in place it may not be as important to."
(Adams, 2017)

"The risk is 'I might have to let go of this perception that has not been serving me.

Healing is risky!

If you stay wounded, you can feel justified. The payoff of taking the risk of healing is wellness." (Blowey, 2013)

What Can I Do?

1. **Be kind.** Many times, it is easy for us to be kinder to others, including the suicide attempter, than it is for us to be kind to ourselves. Many times, it is hard to allow ourselves to feel what we need to because people in our lives tell us we shouldn't feel the way we do. Be kind to yourself.

2. **Don't "should" on yourself.** I had to know it is possible to move on from this and be healthy again. No one told me that, so out of my own fear I didn't want to be honest about my thoughts and feelings. I kept telling myself I <u>should</u> be fine. I *should* have moved on. I shouldn't care. I want to tell you from my research it is possible to be healthy again. You must be honest to work through and walk the path to get there. The best way to be honest is to not *should* all over yourself.

3. **Get help.** Clinical depression is not something to overlook or ignore. This experience, and what surrounds suicide attempts, can cause circumstantial or clinical depression depending on the other situations simultaneously occurring in your life. You can take the hard way or the easier way. It is your choice. I encourage you to get as much help as you can!

4. **Sleep, rest, and meditate.** This is important and goes along with being kind to yourself. These three things are important for your mind and body to recover and process all the events that have occurred.

Workbook

Am I feeling depression as a stage of the grief process or am I experiencing depression, a mental illness?

How will I know when I need help?

Where will I go, if I do need professional help?

What am I afraid of with regards to the grief process and the suicide attempt?

*Fear can be debilitating, what are three actions
I can take to work through my fear?*

Notable Quotes

One common theme I saw emerge was the way many of the interviewees carried on a public persona of "having it all together," even when they were shattered inside. They went to work, did laundry, golfed, cleaned the house, and changed the oil in their vehicle. To the outsider, things looked normal. Most people may not feel a need to check on, or be concerned about them.

I do not know if this is a self-protection reaction so we will not be neglected and hurt again by others if we show we are vulnerable, or if it is simply a way humans carry on during a crisis. I do believe it is another symptom of convoluted grief. When someone's house burns down people know the owner will be upset and most of us know how to help in that grief situation. Maybe, until now, most people don't know how to support people affected by a suicide attempt. Maybe, most people don't know there has been a suicide attempt.

"I didn't function. I cried every day. I felt like I was having heart attacks and that I would die. I felt like my brain belonged to someone else, and no matter how hard I tried, I could not pull myself together enough to get out of the house to go to the store, to make friends or do anything. I let myself feel everything that came

141

and hoped one day I would wake up and feel better. Slowly but surely that is what has happened."

"There seemed to be a lot of things to do and a sense that I had to get a lot of things done. I always felt there was never enough time. I kept myself busy. I could not focus."

"I think I fell apart on a weekly basis for a while, but I think the biggest break down was over Christmas break from college. I started crying like I have never cried before."

"If I was at work, I would leave and go out to my car. I can remember being in the parking lot at work just crying."

"I wasn't the person I had been before. I appeared highly functioning to the outside world because I felt like if I did fall apart, I would lose others' respect. At home I was not functioning."

"I didn't function at all. Other people fed, dressed me, and looked after my family."

Fear of Another Suicide Attempt

Since even one previous attempt multiplies suicide risk by 38-40 times and suicide is the fourth leading cause of death for adults under 65, a proven way to prevent repeat attempts has important public health implications.

Thomas Insel, M.D.,
National Institute for Mental Health Director

For the loved ones of suicide attempt survivors, a universal fear exists: Will the loved one who attempted suicide attempt again? Will I eventually lose my loved one to suicide?

This is yet another way that suicide attempts remain different from other near-death experiences. For example: when a person is in remission from cancer, there is often discussion centering on, "What if it comes back?" This discussion gives the family, friends, and the cancer survivor a chance to plan, ask questions, and a chance to prevent.

After a suicide attempt people do not <u>want</u> to think about, or talk about, the person attempting again. Despite our desire most of us do think about it and fear another attempt. It is difficult to make plans to prevent another attempt because the attempter is still in the midst of the thoughts, emotions and events surrounding the suicide attempt, so our fear is very high and very justified.

It is difficult for loved ones to talk about preventing another attempt for fear of harming the attempter further. It is difficult and necessary.

The truth is, the chances of a second, third, and fourth attempt go up each time the person attempts. Talking about the suicide attempt not only helps to prevent another attempt, but it also helps the loved ones face this fear and deal with it.

"Suicide prevention is people being unafraid to talk about suicide. Being afraid to say 'suicide', perpetuates the heaviness someone might be feeling." (Adams, 2017)

I like to talk about the "tools" we all have in our "tool boxes." When someone gets to the point they attempt suicide, suicide is now a tool in their emotional or mental health tool box. Once that tool is in their tool box, it is obvious from my research, that the tool appears in the tool boxes of those who love them as well.

The key to keeping this a tool that is <u>not</u> used is honest communication. Use of all other "tools," safety plans, support, and professional help.

"30% to 40% of persons who complete suicide have made a previous attempt. The risk of completed suicide is more than 100 times greater than average in the first year after an attempt - 80 times greater for women, 200 times greater for men, 200 times greater for people over 45, and 300 times greater for white men over 65." (Mental Health America, 2017)

When someone has a loved one attempt suicide and that person never attempts again, fear does dissipate quicker than if you have a loved one attempt suicide multiple times. Additionally, fear is increased if attempts happen closely together in time. When there are multiple suicide attempts close in time people I interviewed reported the development of PTSD symptoms and clinical depression at a much higher rate than those who had a loved one attempt suicide once.

"If your suicidal thoughts are not placing you in immediate danger that does not mean you can safely dismiss them.

Shoving those thoughts into a dark corner of your mind and ignoring them has a way of increasing their urgency.

Like mushrooms, suicidal thoughts grow in the dark.

They must be exposed to the light and uprooted, and you may need help to do it.

This is one path you should not try to travel alone." (Mitsch, 1993)

Notable Quotes

"I am most afraid of another suicide attempt or completion."

"I still fear my brother will try to end his life again and fear the guilt and heartache we all felt after the last attempt will come back. Despite thinking we are not all connected, we are. We know we can't do anything to help him until he helps himself, but that is irrelevant when it comes to loss. He has indicated that when he thought it was his time to die he would die. I interpret this to mean that he will again try/succeed in ending his own life."

"I was afraid she'd try suicide again. I just got through each day until I knew my mother (the attempter) knew suicide wasn't the answer."

"That he would try to end his life again and the fear that he will continue to live with such sadness and not be able to live in the moment or share his life or how he feels with those who care about him, is my fear. I have not overcome that, but I no longer live my life in that deep dark shadow."

"Her suicide attempts came during her senior year in high school, and we were terrified about the prospect of her going away to college. We tried to stay in close touch, especially during the first months she was away from home. I think that trusting her to stay in touch, to get help if things began to get emotionally out of hand for her, and then giving her the chance to move on to a new environment and assume some responsibility for her own wellbeing worked out well. But it's frightening."

"My biggest fear was I was going to find him if he completed suicide. My fears became reality."

"I was afraid a suicide attempt would happen again. I am always coming in and making sure that she [the attempter] is still breathing. I am always worried I will get that call. I can't say I have overcome that fear. Thinking about things that might happen is torture and training your mind not to do that is difficult. I feel I am just on edge all of the time."

Stage Five ~ Acceptance and Rebuilding

My grief experience moves with me now. It lives within me. I don't live in the grief anymore.

I can revisit my experience without it being debilitating, that devastating place where it takes over your whole being- when you have your face to the carpet and you can't get up.

I'm no longer paralyzed by it because I choose not to be.

Choosing to "do" your grief work is not an easy path...but choosing to embrace grief rather than separate from it has made for a more profound and enlightened journey.

Carla Blowey

T his stage can be one you resist with every fiber of your being. You may even hear yourself saying things like, "I will never be OK with this." "I will never accept this." "I will never settle in to this new normal." "I will never feel OK." "I won't ever get over this." All these thoughts may come from wanting to honor the person who attempted and honor the love you have for this person. You don't want to ever be OK with having this experience and having someone you love having this experience. I know now that acceptance doesn't mean dishonoring the experience, your love for, or the people involved in this journey.

"Acceptance is often confused with the notion of being 'all right' or 'OK' with what has happened. This is not the case. Most people don't ever feel OK or all right about (a suicide attempt). This stage is about accepting ... this new reality. We will never like this reality or make it OK, but eventually we accept it. We learn to live with it. It is the new norm with which we must learn to live...In resisting this new norm, at first many people want to maintain life as it was before...In time, through bits and pieces of acceptance, however, we see that we cannot maintain the past intact. It has been forever changed and we must readjust. We must learn to reorganize roles, re-assign them to others or take them on ourselves.

Finding acceptance may be just having more good days than bad ones...We can never replace what has been lost, but we can make new connections, new meaningful relationships, new inter-dependencies. Instead of denying our feelings, we listen to our needs; we move, we change, we grow, we evolve. We may start to reach out to others and become involved in their lives. We invest in our friendships and in our relationship with ourselves. We begin to live again, but we cannot do so until we have given grief its time. At times, people in grief will often report more stages. Just remember your grief is as unique as you are."
(Kessler, 2017)

Acceptance for me has been gradual and quiet. My life is now like a young tree planted next to a barbed wire fence. The tree has grown until it is pressing against the fence and the fence is boring its way into the bark and all the way into the soul of the tree. The tree still grows. The tree is still healthy. The tree is still a part of a community and contributing to humanity.

Acceptance for me came by realizing I can incorporate my father's suicide attempts into my life and not have it be my whole life. There were a few years where it was my whole life; it was everything. That was a part of my grief process. Gradually it became less of my life and now it is a piece of the whole. It has modified my life, but I no longer allow it to define me.

154

Remember: It is important to interpret the stages loosely. There is no neat progression from one stage to the next. In reality, there is much looping back, or stages occur at the same time, or occur out of order. So why bother with stage models at all? Because they are a good general guide of what to expect. Outsiders do not understand this, and feel that it should be time for you to 'get over it' and rejoin the land of the living. Just knowing that your desire to be alone with your sad reflections at this time is normal will help you deal with outside pressures. You are acting normally. They just don't 'get it.'" (Wright-Parker, n.d.)

Be kind to yourself and others. This is not a "Do this, and then this, and then you will be fine process."

The things you have lived through are beyond reason and nearly impossible to comprehend.

Ask for help.

Do what is healthy for you.

Realize you may be in every stage of this process at one time.

Be understanding of yourself and others. There is no right way to get through this. The process may never end. I have wonderful days full of laughter, joy and love. I also have dark days full of anxiety, despair and

155

sadness. The wonderful days far outnumber the dark days, now and I am grateful for that.

It is not easy to rebuild, and it certainly does not happen quickly. From my interviews, I learned two years was the average amount of time it took to start to feel like people were moving toward "normalcy" – That is two years from the last suicide attempt.

The grief process is not quick or easy. Sometimes it isn't only depression, anger, or fear that keeps people from accepting what has happened and rebuilding their lives. Many found there were other issues they faced, issues they had never considered prior to this tragedy. During the first two years, people were surprised by other challenges: insurance forms, paperwork, law enforcement, rehabilitation, doctor appointments, gambling, lying, cheating, stealing, and erratic or distrustful behavior on the part of the attempter.

Some people reported the attempter using tobacco, illegal drugs or alcohol when they never had before. The self-destructive actions of a suicide attempt may continue in other self-destructive ways you may not have considered your loved one would ever do prior to the attempt. Another occurrence for some people was having another family member in their life become suicidal. Unfortunately, that fact intensifies the fears, terror, number of doctor appointments and medication you may have to be monitoring. It can also amplify the amount of anger, hopelessness, and PTSD symptoms you may have. **Ask for help**.

After five years, most people reported they felt as good as they think they are going to feel. They have accepted their new reality, rebuilt their life and have found peace and balance. For most, that was the plateau. They had healed as much as they felt they needed to be healthy. You may be different. You may feel great right after the attempt and never feel crazy and hopeless. You may feel hopeless and ashamed immediately and then feel better after a few months.

There is no "normal".

There is the quest to be healthy.

There is nothing you or anyone should expect from you or your grief process.

This time frame question was especially important for me. I didn't know if it was even possible to heal. Two years is a long time, and five years is even longer. That amount of time in your short life can start to feel like forever. It felt to me like my sadness, anger and fear would never reside. It felt to me that I had to accept this unbearable pain as my new reality forever and that was **not ok with me**.

It felt like the tide would never turn.

But it does.

It will for you also.

My hope is you being able to have a time frame where you can start to see small changes is a wonderful tool to have in your tool box.

What Can I Do?

1. **Be honest with your expectations.** Two to five years is a short amount of time if you think about the many kinds of wounds you have survived that need to heal. Two to five years is an incredibly long time when you are under the misunderstanding the wounds will never heal.

2. **Release.** I adore this word.
   I adore this action.
   Release.

   Releasing involves not gripping your pain and fear with your last breath.

   Releasing means just being, not doing.

   Releasing is allowing yourself to breathe, go with the flow and accept yourself and your experience.

   When I am feeling particularly overcome with my fear and obsession of "not letting" I like to do this exercise.

   Grab a chair, a utensil, a tool. Grip it in your hand as hard as you can for a good minute or two.

Your hand will start to go numb.

It will start to feel like you can't release because your hand is cramped and familiar with the feeling of being wrapped around whatever you have chosen.

Now, slowly let go.

Release.

Allow.

Be.

Accept.

3. **Create a ritual.** This step may allow you to feel you aren't actually "OK" with what has happened but allow you to celebrate where you have been and what you have overcome, released, healed from and incorporated in to your new healthier life. Some people release balloons with journal entries tied onto the strings. Some people find a cliff and label rocks with emotions or experiences they then throw away or toss off the cliff.

4. **Be YOU.** You are enough. You are loved. You are accepted. Just be you.

Workbook

How do I move on while honoring my life experience?

What parts of my life need to be rebuilt?

Who can help me in the rebuilding process and what help do I need from them?

What hopes and dreams do I have for my life now?

What do I want my life to feel like going forward?

What are 10 seemingly small action items I can do, daily, if necessary, to create the kind of life I want to experience now?

Notable Quotes

A lot of times we want to know, "What should I do?" Or we hope by asking others what they did, we will find solutions for ourselves. These are great questions to ponder. There are times other people's solutions work incredibly well for many.

I do know life will get better for you. The world did come crashing down on you.

Keep trying.

Keep talking.

Keep loving yourself.

Keep yourself well.

Keep releasing.

Do something every day for your health; mind, body and soul.

Even if it is as simple as going for a walk. Small, seemingly insignificant actions at the time, will add up and you will be healthier for them.

Choose to live your life to the fullest.

Choose healthy behaviors.

Allow yourself to fall apart and lean on those who will let you. You will make new friendships that will be stronger than any you lose. Every day continue to put one foot in front of the other. Every day, move toward being healthy and balanced. Remember some days that movement may mean going back to bed.

"I wish I would have known then that I was going to be ok no matter what. There are people who do love me and who do care. I wish I would have been grateful for them instead of shutting down. Rely on a lot of people. If you only rely on a few people you drain them. If you ask for help from many you have a lot of love coming in from many different areas, many different ways."

"I wish I would have known I would start to not feel anxious and crazy someday. I wish I would have kept a journal. I wish I would have known someday I would stop crying. I wish I would have known someone else who had experienced this. I wish I would have known my distasteful jokes were normal. I wish I would have known the attempter in my life was going to find the humor in the situation, and I wish I would have known how to respond when he did."

"Find an outlet through writing, exercise, anger management, crying, talking, or any creative expression. Just get whatever you are feeling out. Allow yourself to feel what you feel without judging yourself."

"Do not force people to understand what you are going through or try to get them to help you. Hang on to the people who are understanding. Be grateful for them."

"Try and find a level of support – friends, books, and counseling. Make sure you take care of yourself. Make sure you are not alone. You may find yourself searching for answers and not having the kind of control you would like."

"It is so easy to drop into the mode of taking care of everything, especially when the attempter is hospitalized. I did that. I was portrayed as controlling. Forgive yourself. You don't have as much control as you think. It is not about whether you have done the right thing and tried to be there. Ultimately it is about your loved one making the decision to live or die."

"I spent time in nature and accepted every emotion, feeling, and thought as it came. I did not try to sensor anything. I just let it all come. When I did finally lose my mind over all that had happened, I did get help from a doctor. I wish I would not have waited so long trying to handle all of this on my own and trying so hard to be ok."

"Talk to other people. Read. Make sure to take time out and exercise. It will relieve some of the stress that is built up. Writing things down is sometimes helpful. I know when I write thoughts or feelings, it is like I can put my hands around it. I can look at what I am thinking and maybe look at it differently. Then I can burn it, rip it up, or whatever I feel I need to do."

"Talking about the suicide attempt and about my feelings helped me. Stating how I felt about the attempt, not just with other people, but with my wife [the attempter] when she was much healthier. It was helpful that my wife and I could understand what we were each going through and went through."

"I found support mostly with friends and family, a little bit online. Looking back on it I should have sought some form of counseling. That way I could talk about my feelings with someone not entrenched and emotionally involved in the situation."

"I went home to find solace every day from work. We did take one vacation. That was one of the nicest times I have had in my 39 years on this planet. I felt this warm glow around me. Going away with my wife and kids and exploring somewhere new was rejuvenating."

172

"I tend to see the big picture and then break it down. Because my sister [the attempter] wasn't helping herself, was not apologetic, was resentful and in denial, I functioned really well. I was realistic enough to know there wasn't anything I could do. I only fell apart in counseling sessions. I dealt with what I needed to deal with there."

"I screamed in private, went for a walk, exercised, worked in the yard, or did something physical. Physical activity helps to clear my head so I can make good decisions, feel better, or know that maybe I don't have all the right answers, but I am doing good things for myself. Exercise makes me too tired to make any more excuses."

"Setting personal boundaries helped me the most. I set small boundaries to protect me. My family's receptiveness to respecting those boundaries helped also. Knowing I don't want to put the people I love through the same thing [the attempter] put me through, has kept me from thinking self-destructive thoughts."

"Talking about my feelings and thoughts incessantly seemed to help me the most. Telling and retelling the story and the events and everything surrounding the suicide attempt, and how I felt about it, whether others agreed or not, was something I had to do. I meditated and read. I take an hour for me every day with no TV, radio, telephone or noise."

"As a family, we went to a therapy session. It was helpful to have someone from the outside listen to us and help us talk through what happened."

"I don't think there was any one person who helped the most. It was a community effort and people were lending an ear and listening. They didn't try to fix the situation or change it. They just listened."

"If I could have gotten some validation that I am doing the right thing. Even better, if I am not doing the right thing, tell me what I need to do. Attempted suicide is such an unnerving event that criticizing and questioning from other people doesn't help. Positive feedback and answers would be better. I wish I could understand what I was doing that was so wrong. The interpersonal dynamic surrounding suicide and suicide attempts is hurtful."

Notable Quotes - What May Stall Your Recovery

There may be words, actions, or other people who temporarily halt your healing process. This does not have to be a permanent set back. The following are things others experienced that either harmed them, or made it difficult for them to move forward.

If you are supporting someone affected by a suicide attempt, please refrain from any of the following.

If you are affected by a suicide attempt and have these things happen to you know you are not alone and other people have experienced this and still healed with time.

"The people who brought up religious references to God, the Devil, Satan, Hell, etc. definitely were destructive. **Do not use religion as a weapon**."

"People who admitted later they forgot the attempter had shot himself. I still cannot comprehend forgetting something like that."

"Some of the professional help I received was definitely not helpful. Some family and friend's advice was unsolicited and unhelpful. My behavior, and just plain not knowing what to do, was very unhelpful to me and everyone around me."

"When you meet someone who has lost a loved one to suicide, it is hurtful when they judge you and are angry at you because your loved one is alive. I don't believe I will ever get over that."

"The risky behavior after his attempts and him joking about his suicide attempts is hurtful. Walking on egg shells is hard enough without the repeated threats to do it again. His words and actions always made me second guess myself."

Expect to Get Professional Help

You need to find a balance between "saving" your loved one and letting your loved one face natural consequences of his or her actions. You will need professional help, not only for you, but for your loved one. Get help to figure out this fine balance.

For me, the process of finding and affording professional help was difficult. I live in a rural area with few affordable mental health professionals. With my mind clouded by depression I could not see I needed professional help. You may find this same experience. You may be like people I interviewed who found compassionate, caring, prompt, professional help that propelled them quickly through their healing process.

Some professionals are going to be a good fit. Some will not. When you find someone to work with you please keep some standards, hopes, and goals for your professional relationship in the forefront of your mind. If you are not finding or receiving what you need search out another professional. Don't stop until you are getting the treatment you need. Don't give up.

You may not think you need help at all. That is your choice. I can tell you suicide attempters need professional help. They need to deal with all the thoughts, emotions, situations, and feelings that led to the attempt. Those situations may include mental illness, chemical imbalances, abuse, and neglect. They must get quality professional help. You may need to help seek it for them. It does need to be a part of their safety plan and one of the tools they use for their own healing process.

The problem I have seen with not receiving quality professional help is that people tend to lean very heavily on the people who were strongly affected by the suicide attempt. I believe this happens because they are the only people we know who understand what we are going through.

However, when you choose this path you have no guidance for good boundaries and ways to heal. When you are speaking with other wounded members of your close family, or group, wounds can get re-opened. Other wounds may be inflicted. This occurs, not out of spite, but because no one can monitor what is healthy. I can't tell you the number of times we had conversations in our family about whether we were unintentionally harming each other; if we should not speak about the attempt and if we should set boundaries to not vent to each other. The problem was, we didn't have anyone else. We had to use, and sometimes misused each other just to make it through the day. I don't recommend stumbling through this without serious quality professional help for everyone involved.

"When family members chose to not

get professional help after a suicide attempt they are choosing, suffering.

People that chose help chose not to suffer.

The consequences of not seeking help are sacrificing your happiness, sacrificing your relationships.

You are choosing suffering. You are choosing to not be authentic, you are not being free." (Cooper, 2012)

Expectations After a Suicide Attempt

After a suicide attempt in a family the truth may come out. The attempt produces what has been covert – secrets, alliances, agreements, loyalties, betrayals, guilt, shame, helplessness, powerlessness, mortality.
IT BRINGS OUT the state of affairs of our relationships which is another level of grief and loss issues.

(Cooper, 2012)

A person can't cause someone to try to kill themselves any more than they could cause someone to have heart disease. We are all responsible for our own actions and our own decisions.

(Bryan, 2012)

The First 72 Hours

What to Expect

- Feelings of guilt, shame, fear, sleeplessness, hopelessness, shock, disbelief, betrayal, frustration, sadness, rage, anger, emptiness.
- Loss of appetite.
- Blame from close family, friends, professionals or first responders.
- Insecurity – You may not know what is happening or what to tell people.
- Feeling uneasy or jumpy.
- The suicide attempter asking you to promise you won't tell anyone. **If this happens <u>do not</u> make this promise. Seek help for yourself and the attempter.**
- Blame from the suicide attempter.
- Difficulty falling asleep or staying asleep.
- Nightmares.
- The need to deal with law enforcement, insurance companies, doctors, nurses, and hospital personnel.
- A wish that the attempter had ended his/her life.
- Loss of religious faith.
- A dark sense of humor.
- The attempter may be released from the hospital to your care. Make sure you have a list of medications and know how to give them, names of doctors and nurses you can call if needed and an appointment with doctors to follow up with the attempter.

- A desire for an apology from the suicide attempter.
- Feeling isolated or alone.
- Being critical of yourself and your actions.
- Increased irritability and angry outbursts.
- Relief, that you are not to blame and that there is a medical explanation.
- Relief, that you have resources and others may finally know what you have been privately dealing with.
- Hope that you may have more support now.
- Validation that there is something wrong.

What You Need to Do

- Drink lots of water. Carry a water bottle with you everywhere.
- Buy a notebook and pen. Write down everything in it. You may think you will remember what you have been told about appointments, doctors' names, and diagnosis of the attempter, but you will not.
- Call for an appointment with a therapist for you and your family members. It may be weeks before you can be seen.
- Call for a therapist appointment for all children affected by the suicide attempt.
- Eat fresh fruits and vegetables.
- At a minimum, go for short walks.
- Breathe. Take long deep breaths.
- Talk. Talk. Talk.
- Be honest. Express your thoughts, feelings and emotions honestly.
- Ask for help.
- Remove all means of self-harm from your residence for now. There should not be access to guns, knives, medication, ropes, razors, alcohol, etc.
- Work with the attempter to create a safety plan for the attempter.
- Use positive mantras as a tool.
- Be kind to yourself and take excellent care of yourself.

- Program the number 1-800-273-8255 into your cell phone and the cell phone of the attempter. It is The National Suicide Prevention Lifeline and is 24- hour resource. The lifeline does help callers who are non-English speaking. SuicidePreventionLifeline.org

The First Month

What to Expect

- Your relationships with yourself and others will change.
- People who said they would be there may not be.
- You may want to discount your own fears about the suicide attempt or others fears.
- You may have family and friends who remain very loyal to you but are angry and say very hurtful things about the suicide attempter.
- Extreme amounts of stress.
- Changes in sleep patterns and dream patterns.
- You may not be able to cry or you may not be able to stop crying.
- Loss of appetite.
- Inability to concentrate or remember simple math or the spelling of simple words.
- You may face a lot of anger from people who have lost a loved one to suicide.
- You may still be dealing with police and the first responders to your loved one's suicide attempt. They may be continuing to ask questions to finish filing reports.
- Your loved one may be hospitalized, either voluntarily, or involuntarily.

What You Need to Do

- Buckle your seat belt. Turn on your head lights. Double check everything while you drive and don't drive if you don't need to. Allow someone else to drive you where you need to go for a while. It is common for people affected by a suicide attempt to be in a car accident and/or be pulled over for forgetting simple things like turn signals, stop signs and headlights.
- Turn off your phone while driving. You do not need any distractions what so ever.
- Learn who you can rely on for support, encouragement, a listening ear, and friendship.
- Set personal boundaries.
- Ask for help.
- Set up a regular exercise routine.
- Set up a minimum of 30-minute daily meditation time.
- Be honest.
- Be patient.
- Accept whatever thoughts and feelings come to you.
- Stick to a regular bedtime routine.
- Eat well.
- Don't give up.
- Continue counseling.

- Find 6 – 10 people you can count on. The larger safety net you weave around yourself the easier it will be and the healthier you will be.
- You need to check in with, and advocate on behalf of, the children affected by the suicide attempt.
- Ask the attempters' doctor what they believe the attempter is capable of physically and mentally.
- Record all the names of professionals attending to your loved one.
- If you are having thoughts about suicide or feelings of despair create a safety plan for yourself, either alone, or with the help of your mental health professional.

What Can I Do for the Attempter?

- Accept the person for who he/she is.
- Ask what responsibilities he/she would like.
- Help him/her write a safety plan, if that hasn't been done yet.
- Assist in writing a Daily List of things they would like to accomplish. These can be simple like "go for a walk around the block;" "feed the dog;" "brush and floss my teeth."
- Be in control of their medications.
- Help set personal goals and family goals.
- Plan things to look forward to – daytrips, celebrations, cookouts, birthdays, graduations, and other events.

What Should I NOT Say to Someone Who Has Attempted Suicide?

- "Why did you do this to me?"
- "Do you know how bad this hurts me?"
- "What were you thinking?"
- "Do you know how bad this is going to make me look?"
- "How could you do this to me?"
- "What is wrong with you?"
- "I can't do anything to help you."
- "You have so much good in your life."
- "Stop acting so crazy."
- "It is all in your head."
- "Why would you want to do this?"
- "Just get over it."
- "Whatever made you do it?"
- "When are you going to get better?"
- "Shouldn't you be better by now?"
- "Snap out of it."
- "Pull yourself together."
- "We all have hard times."
- "You'll be fine."
- "Look on the bright side."

- "Pull yourself up by the bootstraps."
- "Your life is not that bad."
- "You have so much to live for."
- "Think of all the things you have to be grateful for."
- "Did you even stop to consider all the people who care about you?"
- "You are so selfish."
- "You should feel bad for all of the people's lives you have affected by this."

What to Say to the Attempter

Offer support, understanding and love. If that is not possible excuse yourself from the situation or that person's life.

Do Say:
- "I am not sure how to help you but I will stay with you."
- "I am here for you, and we will get through this together."
- "You are not alone."
- "You are important to me."
- "I am here for you."
- "Tell me how I can help you now."
- "Your life is important to me."
- "I may not know exactly how you feel but I do care about you and want to help you."

The First Six Months

What to Expect

- Wondering when you are going to feel like normal.
- Fear of a second attempt.
- Feeling run down and abandoned.
- Anger at everyone and everything.
- Needing to talk incessantly about what you have been through.
- The attempter may promise they will never attempt again. They may tell you what they have learned or give you reasons why they will never attempt again. This does not mean they will not re-attempt and does not mean you will not fear a future suicide attempt.
- Fear and resentment.
- People saying they will never trust the attempter again and will never allow their loved ones around the attempter.
- People may tell you the attempter didn't really want to die. You may hear that the attempter just wanted attention, or it was a cry for help.
- Confusion about religion and God.

What You Can Do

- Ensure the attempter is taking all prescribed medications properly and regularly.
- Take care of yourself.
- Talk.
- Continue to see your therapist.
- Breathe.
- Exercise.
- Be honest.
- Eat healthy food.
- Drink water.
- Meditate.
- Rest and sleep.
- Enforce boundaries you have set.

A Network of Support

How Can I Help My Friend?

If you are a friend, spouse or relative of someone who has experienced a suicide attempt of a loved one, you will hear a lot about the attempt, its effects, and the feelings and thoughts your friend has. Some of what you hear may make no sense to you. Listen to your loved one and love them where they are. You cannot set a time and date for the healing process to be over. Sometimes helping your loved one find a professional counselor to speak to will be the most important step you take. If your friend looks fine they may be on auto pilot and really need help or support in finding professional help, including help with daily tasks or other things. Ask!

"It's impossible to tell someone how to grieve. You can help someone but never instruct them." (Doka, 2000)

Listen and be kind. Do not pretend the suicide attempt did not happen. Offer help – child care, an afternoon or evening alone or with you, a car wash or lawn mowing, or a hot dinner. Drop by and care for pets. Set a day you will pick up their kids from school and keep them through dinner, and possibly help with homework. Check in often. Let the person express what he or she is going through without censoring or judging what you hear. Drop a note in the mail. Leave voice messages to say, "I care about you." Do not expect a return phone call. These kind actions may be needed and appreciated for up to two years following the attempt.

Another great way to be a support of someone who had a family member, or close friend, attempt suicide is to offer to be the main contact person. Volunteer to call or email close friends or relatives with pertinent updates to the physical and emotional well-being of all loved ones involved. Schedule visits, meals, child and pet care, etc. There is no "right" person for this job. A great person is a willing person who can communicate honestly with everyone involved.

Notable Quotes - What People Needed the Most

"Just let me talk. Let me talk about it. Let me talk about it over and over."

"Listen and pray for us."

"The people who were just there to play tennis with me and would just leave it at that helped. The people who didn't pry and didn't share their opinions about suicide with me helped me. I didn't need anyone's opinion on this."

"The thing that did the most for me was the people that got together and asked what they could do and then followed through with action."

"They made it possible for me to grieve as long as I wanted. I knew my children were being looked after by the people helping us so there was no set time limit I had to grieve and move on by."

"I would have liked to have had more support. It would have been helpful if people would have called just to see how I was doing."

"I wish people would have let me know they were thinking about me. I wish they would have just called to check in and see how I was or if there was anything I needed without being judgmental."

"Listened and not given advice. Called or asked what they could do. Not acted sometimes as if we must have done something wrong to make our loved one want to die."

"I wish I would have been given me more time to deal with it. It felt like people just expected me to move on and be ok within a couple of days."

"I wish people would have been more aggressive in doing small things for [the attempter's] family. One woman took his wife [the attempter's] shopping and got her new clothes for work and she was like a teenage girl. She was so excited."

"Call and tell someone what you are going to do. Don't ask. Call and say I am coming over to mow the yard."

"Listen, share, offer support, seek to gain greater understanding of depression and the other causes of suicide."

"I would send notes in the mail. Call them and just let them talk. I would ask them what they needed and then follow through."

"I think the more specific you are the better. I would not say, 'I am here if you want to talk.' I say, 'Let's meet at Starbucks at 4:00 on Thursday.' 'I am making dinner at 5:00 on Saturday. Please come over.'"

"I would listen to what is going on. I would take them for walks while they talk. Exercise is always nice. Say to them, 'Let's talk again.' Hand them a phone number. Set up something. Get contacts for them and for other places to get help and support. Make sure they are doing things to take care of themselves."

Suicide Attempts and Children

Every family member is damaged by the family's inability to deal effectively with mental illness...Since mental illness affects everyone in the family – siblings, children, parents, and spouses – answers must be found for everyone, not only for the one who is mentally ill.

(Tallard Johnson, 1988)

One of the biggest challenges many loved ones of suicide attempters face is: "What do I tell the children?" While working through your own disbelief and questions there are many questions children also have. The age of the children and the relation or relationship to the attempter may change how you handle telling them.

Perhaps you feel your children are at an age where knowing about a suicide attempt in the family will do more harm than good or will make them consider suicide themselves? Perhaps you are the parent of adult children who have their own families and their own issues, and you don't want to "burden them" with your challenges? Maybe the children are young, and were in the home at the time of the attempt, so witnessed the event, the EMT's and the clean up?

Realizing time is a factor and waiting for a therapist appointment may not be possible, I would strongly suggest this is a time to seek professional guidance. Children of any age will notice changes in you. Your emotions may be on the surface. They may notice your lack of patience. They will overhear conversations, even when you believe they can't. Be sure children have a safe person, or people, such as a professional counselor, to speak to openly about their feelings. You need to decide if you will tell the children's' teachers, *their friends' parents, etc. A professional can help you determine how and when to do this.*

Research suggests being as honest as possible with children in this situation is most healthy. You can be honest and say things like:

- "Your aunt is in the hospital."
- "We don't know if he will be ok."
- "I am here for you."
- "I love you."
- "I know you have questions and we will work through this together."
- "There are things I don't feel you are old enough to know right now and I am going to protect you until you are a bit older."

Do not say, "Everything is going to be fine," "It is not a big deal," and "Don't worry." It is a big deal and it is also very normal for everyone affected to have concerns and to be worried. When you tell children something is not a big deal, which is a big deal to them it creates confusion, mistrust, and conflict.

"It's important that parents and adults are honest with children, even if they want to protect them." (Linn-Gust, 2007)

"Picture your family as a mobile, with each part in careful balance with the other, moving together with the different air flow. Now imagine someone has removed or greatly disturbed one part-all the other parts move in reaction to it. In the same way, a suicide attempt affects the entire family." (Bryan, 2012)

Per Sean Brotherson, Ph.D., and April Anderson, parent educator, from their published document Talking to Children About Suicide (FS637):

"Suicide is not a comfortable topic. It is sobering, serious and saddening to talk about. But the factors involved in suicide and approaches to diminishing or preventing its occurrence must be openly talked about in responsible ways. Silence cannot prevent the problem of suicide – it only can make it worse. Understanding when, how, why and who should talk about suicide is important...When approaching the topic of suicide, distinguishing among suicidal ideation (thoughts about suicide), suicide attempts (efforts to injure oneself that can result in death) and completed suicide can be important.

Children or adolescents who think about or discuss suicide is most common, and suicide attempts are much more common than completed suicides. Suicide rates for young people ages 10 to 24, both males and females, declined gradually from 1994 to 2007, but increased significantly from 2007 to 2013.

Generally, the average person may have a difficult time comprehending the thoughts of a suicidal person. Small issues may seem a looming monster to a person contemplating suicide. If a child or adolescent is considering suicide, providing him or her with professional help is essential. Suicide cannot be dealt with inside a closed family unit. Improving the situation generally will take a family effort, and professional counseling and assistance.

Talking to Young Children (ages 4 to 8)
When talking to young children from ages 4 to 8:
What to Say and Do
• Talk with young children about their feelings. Help them label their feelings so they will better understand and be more aware of what is going on inside them. You might ask: "How are you feeling? Are you feeling sad or angry? Do you feel sad or angry only once in awhile or do you feel it a lot of the time?"

• Encourage young children to express their feelings. Talking to them helps to strengthen the connection between them and you. It also lets them know they can share feelings safely with adults they know. Teach that feelings of hurt and anger can be shared with others who can understand and give support.

• If a child does not seem to feel comfortable expressing feelings verbally, support other ways to express feelings, such as writing, drawing or being

216

physically active. Give young children healthy ways to express themselves and work through feelings.

• Explain to young children that being sad from time to time is normal. Sadness is the emotion people feel in times of loss, disappointment or loneliness. Teach children that talking about feeling sad or angry, and even shedding tears or being upset, is OK. Be clear that they should talk to others or do something else when feeling sad, but should not seek to harm themselves in any way.

• Take steps to ensure that young children do not have easy access to materials they could use to harm themselves. Be certain knives, pills and particularly firearms are inaccessible to all children.

• Focus on active involvement with young children that provides them with a focus for their feelings and energies. Play games, participate in sports, visit playgrounds and do other activities together. Stay closely connected to them so you can intervene and provide support if necessary.

Talking to Adolescents (ages 9 to 13)
When talking to adolescents from ages 9 to 13:
What to Say and Do
• Be aware of depression and its symptoms in adolescent children. Depression often does not go away on its own and is linked to risk of suicide when it lasts

217

for periods of two weeks or more. Talk with individuals who have knowledge of depression in children to further understand the symptoms and how to intervene.

• Adolescents have many stressors in their lives and sometimes consider suicide as an escape from their worries or feelings. Be aware of your adolescent's stressors and talk with him or her about them. Let your child know you care and emphasize that "suicide is not an option; help is always available." Suicide is a permanent choice.

• Assist adolescents so they don't become overwhelmed with negative thoughts, which can lead to thoughts of suicide. Help them learn to manage negative thinking and challenge thoughts of hopelessness. If needed, treatment or therapy can help an adolescent deal with negative thoughts.

• Emphasize that alcohol and drugs are not a helpful source of escape from the stressors of an adolescent's life. An adolescent who is suffering from depression and also turns to alcohol and drugs is at a greater risk of attempting suicide.

• Be attentive to risk factors in an adolescent's life, as suicide is not always planned at younger ages. Recognizing the warning signs that might be leading to suicide is important.

• Encourage adolescents to talk about and express their feelings. Provide a listening ear and be a support so they can visit with you about how they feel. Adolescents deal much better with tough circumstances when they have at least one person who believes in them.

Talking to Teens (ages 14 to 18)
When talking to teens from ages 14 to 18:
What to Say and Do
• Recognize the signs and symptoms of depression in teens. These may include feelings of sadness, excessive sleep or inability to sleep, weight loss or gain, physical and emotional fatigue, continuing anxiety, social withdrawal from friends or school, misuse of drugs or alcohol and related symptoms. Intervene and get professional help and resources if necessary.

• Ask teens about what they are feeling, thinking and doing. Open communication helps teens talk freely about their concerns and seek support. Make yourself available to talk with teens often. Avoid being critical or judgmental; listen, don't immediately "fix" the problem.

• Provide support if a teen expresses thoughts related to suicide or shares stories of suicide attempts. Stay with him or her and seek additional help. Guide the teen to professional therapists who can give assistance.

• Listen to teens and pay attention to language related to hurting themselves or others, wanting to "go away" or "just die," or similar ideas. Such expressions always should be taken seriously. Respond with support for the teen and access resources to provide further counseling or guidance.

• Encourage teens to be attentive to their peers and quickly report to a respected adult any threats, direct or indirect, that suggest the possibility of suicide. Teens often are aware of such threats among their peers before others and can serve to support peers and provide resources. Talk about the idea that being a true friend means not keeping secrets that could lead to someone being dead.

Helping children cope with suicide attempts can be difficult. During this time, it is important to remember the following points:

• Be open and communicate at a child's level of understanding.

• Share your thoughts and feelings by letting them see your tears or help them know that expressing their sadness is OK.

• Be honest with your children and give correct information in a loving, compassionate way.

• Talk about the (suicide attempter) in sensitive ways.

• Discuss better ways than suicide to handle problems that may occur.

- Assist children and youth to process the shock and emotion they may feel when a suicide (attempt) occurs.
- Allow children who have experienced such loss to connect through talking, writing a journal, prayer or meditation, looking at pictures or other means." (Brotherson, 2016)

Siblings, especially younger ones, may not understand, and get lost or overlooked in the intense focus on depressed and suicidal teenagers.

Some attention on siblings can bring a lot of healing to them and become an added relief for families...Families must work at staying healthy by balancing their routines, engaging in healthy eating, sleeping and exercising patterns, staying socially connected, and participating in family therapy. (Gerali, 2009)

Notable Quotes

"My daughter's younger brother and sister were told but I would do that differently. I would make sure they got the help they needed."

"At the time my son was 3; the attempter's sons were 2 and 8. My son looked up to her [the attempter's] older son and wanted to know why we couldn't see them. I told my son his friends' mom was sick and that we would go and see them soon. I don't know what else I could have told him. I wouldn't want to bring the idea of suicide into his little 3-year-old world, but I did have to tell him some reason why we weren't going over there for a while. I guess that was the best thing I could come up with."

"I told them the absolute truth in a language they could understand for their age at the time. 'Your father is in so much pain he thought it was best for all of us that he would not be here.' I didn't ever talk bad about their dad to them or to anyone. I believe that the truth, however you have to tell it, is important to children's healing and understanding. Leaving children with doubt when everything is so crazy is cruel."

"I told the children we would work through the situation and do everything possible to heal the hurts."

"I didn't tell them based on her [the attempter's] request. We didn't know who she would be when she got out of the hospital. We didn't know what to expect. My own issues became more about 'How do I help my children?' I had to become the dad, the strong one, the one that would be there. Later I had to deal with all of my stuff surrounding the suicide attempt."

"I told my son what had happened. I wouldn't change that. My son is 12. I told my daughter that there was an accident. She just turned 7. I told my daughter her uncle had been drinking and there was an accident."

"I told my kids Grandpa was in the hospital and we didn't know if he was going to be OK. When he overdosed, I told them he had a stomach ache and was really sick. When he shot himself, I told them he had a bad headache. I know my oldest son, age 10, knew I wasn't telling him the whole truth, but he didn't ask a lot of questions because I think he knew I was protecting him. I did tell him about a year later when we knew Grandpa was going to be OK. I think at the time we didn't know if my dad would live or die, and so I was as vague but as truthful as possible. All three of my children know about the attempts now. It is a fact of their life. My daughter, age 7, asked me on the way to school 'Why would Grandpa want to shoot himself?'

"Grieving is a necessary passage and a difficult transition to finally letting go of sorrow - it is not a permanent rest stop." Anonymous

---

What to Do If Someone Is Suicidal

T his section begins with a list of warning signs, or thing to look for, if you think someone may be struggling with suicidal thoughts or actions.

WARNING SIGNS OF DEPRESSION
The following symptoms have been organized into broad categories for easier reference. It is important to note not all symptoms will be experienced by an individual and not all symptoms have to occur for a person to want to die or attempt to end their life. Depression is a treatable disease.

CHANGES IN ACTIVITY OR ENERGY LEVEL
- decreased energy
- fatigue
- lethargy
- diminished activity
- insomnia or hypersomnia
- loss of interest in pleasurable activities
- social withdrawal
- staying up all night
- massive increase in energy level and thoughts

PHYSICAL CHANGES
- unexpected aches and pains
- weight loss or weight gain
- decreased appetite or increased appetite
- psychomotor agitation or retardation

- being clumsy, accident prone, excessive bruising
- sudden, drastic changes in hair color, body modification or clothes style
- cutting and evidence of bodily self-harm
- Increase use of alcohol or drugs

EMOTIONAL PAIN
- prolonged sadness
- unexplained, uncontrollable crying
- feelings of guilt
- feelings of worthlessness
- loss of self-esteem
- despair
- hopelessness/helplessness
- anxiety
- fearful
- withdrawing or feeling isolated
- feeling hopeless and having no reason to live

DIFFICULT MOODS
- irritability/ impatient
- anger
- rage
- worry/anxiety
- pessimism
- indifference
- self-critical

- experiencing any combination of the above and then suddenly appearing healthy and "back to normal"
- extreme mood swing
- reckless behavior

CHANGES IN THOUGHT PATTERNS
- inability to concentrate
- memory loss, or changes
- indecision
- changes in ability to reason, spell, or complete basic math
- disorganized
- forgetful

PREOCCUPATION WITH DEATH
- thoughts of death
- talk of death or others "being better off without them"
- suicidal ideation
- feeling dead or detached
- saying good bye to people they are close to
- giving away possessions they care deeply about
- getting their affairs in order
- reading, talking and thinking about all forms of death
- Looking for a way to kill oneself (online searches)

If Someone You Love is Having Suicidal Thoughts

There is help and hope. I know you are anxious, scared, and worried. Here are some things you need to do and answers to some questions you may have.

"The first rule of suicide intervention is *do something!* Don't stop to worry about doing something wrong. It's doing nothing that gets people killed. Bear in mind that the suicidal, or possibly suicidal, person with whom you're dealing is still with us, so at least part of him or her wants to live. Trust me on this: The part that wants to live is more forgiving of our missteps as interventionists and therapists than you might imagine. So go ahead. Take the first steps." (Quinnett, 2009)

"Ask the question

If you are uncertain whether a person is having suicidal thoughts, the simplest and most effective way to find out is to ask in a direct, kind manner. It may be difficult, but this question, more than anything else that might be said, has the potential to save a life. Asking this question will *not* put the idea in someone's mind. To the contrary, it is most often a relief for the suicidal individual to know he can finally talk about his secret to someone who will listen. He has now been given direct permission to speak the unspeakable.

There are many ways in which to ask this crucial question. A few suggestions follow:

- I am wondering if you ever think of ending your life.
- Sometimes people who are going through what you are now think about suicide. Are you thinking of suicide?
- Have you been having suicidal thoughts?
- Are you thinking of killing yourself?

How *not* to ask the question:
- You're not thinking of suicide, are you?
- You aren't thinking of doing something stupid, are you?
- You aren't thinking of hurting yourself, are you?

Asking in a negative way may tell the person that you do not want to hear the truth or may not be capable of listening to his truthful answer. Using the word hurt leaves on 'out' for the person to deny suicidal thoughts, as he is not thinking of just 'hurting' himself, but of killing himself. Best not to take that chance." (Cobain & Larch, 2006)

Do not leave your loved one alone. If they are not in the same geographic location as you, find someone to go to them and stay with them. This is a non-negotiable. This is not just for an hour. You may need to stay with them for a few days. Feeling isolated is one of the many things people who are having suicidal thoughts report feeling. You may feel isolated while trying to help them also. Do not give up.

Remove all means of causing harm and death. If there are guns, take them and put them somewhere safe and locked where they can't be accessed. Remove all pills, alcohol, drugs, razors, knives, ropes, string, twine, and take away car keys, etc. While you are in crisis and concerned, you must use common sense and realize you don't want to lose your loved one and they most likely do not want to die. They just want the pain they are in to cease.

Call for help. 1-800-273-TALK in the US is answered by live people and they will patch you through to resources in your geographic area. They are there to listen, provide resources, and help. There are a lot of suicide prevention organizations, and you are the bridge to help your loved one get the help they need. Ask for help. Call local resources, doctors, therapists or people you trust. I can assure you without a doubt in my soul that there are so many people who will do whatever it takes to help you and to help keep your loved one alive until they can feel mentally well again. I will also assure you there are many people who will dismiss you and your loved one and be hurtful and unhelpful. Do not give up.

One question we all ask in this situation is: "Will the person who is having suicidal thoughts be mad at me for telling someone?" They may be angry with you. They may say very hurtful public things about how you are not trustworthy and no longer their friend and how you don't really care about them. That is a risk we all take. When everything is resolved, you may end up not being friends anymore. You may not be as close as you were for some time after this event. Whatever happens, when you look back on this time you will feel better if you are confident you did all you could for the person you love, no matter the outcome.

For information on a safety plan and tools go to: http://www.comh.ca/publications/resources/pub_cwst/C WST.pdf

---

"You are not your feelings. We must strive to operate with emotional intelligence.

Often people operate from their emotions which leads to chaos because our emotions are unpredictable.

Awareness allows us to use our morals to make decisions. You are not always going to feel this way. You don't become your feelings!" (Cooper, 2012)

Conclusion

Perhaps just the knowledge that our survival instinct is strong, and that a great many have not only endured terrible losses but have also thrived can be a source of hope, something that I found to be quite scarce in our grief culture.

(Davis Konigsberg, 2011)

These resources for loved ones are critical. It is critical they have options. It is as important as us choosing not to suffer. Choices that are competent. People want to get better but when we don't have resources we suffer and are helpless and powerless. There must be resources, outreach, interaction and relationships so people don't feel isolated.

(Cooper, 2012)

You will survive and you can thrive. It will take time. It will take effort. I hope you will choose to use this experience to better your life and the lives of those you love. You will be able to laugh, love, and feel something other than fear and despair again. You are not alone.

Here are some mantras you may find useful as you move forward in your healing:

"My life is the only one I am responsible for.

My life is a gift.

I free myself from all guilt and judgment. I am not a victim of this tragedy.

I will grow from this experience.

Grief mixed with love always works.

Grief mixed with love always heals.

I forgive myself for everything I think I did not do.

I forgive myself for everything I did that I judged I should not have done.

I forgive myself completely for everything.

I recognize that only the love is real.

I recognize my own worth.

I am loveable no matter what happens in the world.

My soul's worth is always of value.

My relationships are sacred.

I am responsible for my own soul's journey.

My life is the only one I am responsible for.

My life is a gift.

I free myself from all guilt and judgment." (Hay & Kessler, 2014)

For more information visit <u>AttemptedSuicideHelp.com</u>. The website will be continually updated with research, information, gifts of support, resources, and inspiration.

Works Cited

Adams, A. L. (2017, February 15). Professional experience counseling suicide attempters and their loved ones. (J. K. Carr, Interviewer)

Aiger, A. (2015, November 18). *The Bargaining Stage of Grief*. Retrieved February 13, 2017, from Livestrong: http://www.livestrong.com/article/143100-the-bargaining-stage-grief/

American Foundation for Suicide Prevention. (n.d.). Retrieved January 31, 2017, from American Foundation for Suicide Prevention: https://afsp.org/about-suicide/suicide-statistics/

Beaumont, L. R. (2009). Retrieved February 2, 2017, from Emotional Competency: http://www.emotionalcompetency.com/anger.htm

Blowey, C. (2013, February 22). Do People Grieve After A Suicide Attempt? (J. K. Carr, Interviewer)

Brotherson, S. P. (2016, February). *Talking to Children About Suicide*. Retrieved February 2, 2017, from North Dakota State University: https://www.ag.ndsu.edu/publications/kids-family/talking-to-children-about-suicide

Bryan, H. B. (2012). *After An Attempt: The Emotional Impact of a Suicide Attempt on Families.*

Harrisburg, Pennsylvania, United States: PreventSuicidePA.org.

Cobain, B., & Larch, J. (2006). *Dying to Be Free.* City Center, Minnesota, United States: Hazelden.

Cooper, E. L. (2012, September). Are Resources Necessary for Loved Ones? (J. K. Carr, Interviewer)

Davis Konigsberg, R. (2011). *The Truth About Grief.* New York, New York, United States : Simon and Schuster.

Doka, K. J. (2000). *Living with Grief; Children, Adolescents, and Loss.* United States: Routledge.

Ellis, T. M. (2006). *This Thing Called Grief.* Minneapolis, Minnesota: Syren Book Company.

Gerali, S. P. (2009). *What Do I Do When Teenagers are Depressed and Contemplate Suicide.* Grand Rapids, Michigan, United States: Zondervan.

Hay, L., & Kessler, D. (2014). *You Can Heal Your Heart.* Carlsbad, California, United States: Hay House. Retrieved February 13, 2017

Hospice Foundation of America. (1997). *Living with Grief When Illness is Prolonged.* (K. J. Doka, Ed.) Rutledge.

IMDb.com Inc. (2017, January 31). *IMDB Adam Arkin.* Retrieved from Internet Movie Data Base: http://www.imdb.com/name/nm0035060/

Kessler, D. (2017, January 31). *The Five Stages of Grief.* Retrieved January 31, 2017, from Grief: http://grief.com/the-five-stages-of-grief/

Kubler-Ross, E. M. (2014). *On Grief and Grieving.* New York, New York, United States: Simon & Schuster.

Linn-Gust, M. (2007). *Do They Have Bad Days In Heaven?* Albuquerque, New Mexico, United States: Chellehead Works.

Mason, P. T., & Kreger, R. (1998). *Stop Walking on Eggshells.* Oakland, California, United States: New Harbinger Publications, Inc. Retrieved February 13, 2017

Melinda Smith, M. a. (2017, January 20). *Coping with Grief and Loss.* Retrieved from Helpguide: https://www.helpguide.org/articles/grief-loss/coping-with-grief-and-loss.htm

Mental Health America. (2017). Retrieved February 13, 2017, from MentalHealthAmerica.net: http://www.mentalhealthamerica.net/suicide

Mitsch, R. R. (1993). *Grieving the Loss of Someone You Love.* Ann Arbor, Michigan, United States: Servant Publications.

Price, E. (1983). *Getting Through the Night.* New York: Ballantine Books.

Quinnett, P. G. (2009). *Counseling Suicidal People.* Spokane, Washington: QPR Institute.

Rand, M. (1985). *Free To Grieve.* Minneapolis: Bethany House Publishers.

Shantz Hertzler, J. (2017, January 31). *Journey Through Grief Grief Quotes*. Retrieved January 31, 2017, from Journey Through Grief: http://www.journey-through-grief.com/grief-quotes.html

Tallard Johnson, J. M. (1988). *Hidden Victims Hidden Healers.* Edina, Minnesota, United States: PEMA Publications, Inc.

The National Institute of Mental Health (NIMH) is part of the National Institutes of Health (NIH), a component of the U.S. Department of Health and Human Services. (n.d.). Retrieved January 31, 2017, from National Insitiute of Mental Health: https://www.nimh.nih.gov/health/statistics/suicide/index.shtml

Vatner, J. (2009, February 1). *Mourning Becomes Neglected: 4 Healthy Ways to Grieve.* Retrieved January 31, 2017, from Oprah: http://www.oprah.com/health/Healthy-Ways-to-Mourn-Disenfranchised-Grief

Wright-Parker, J. R.-C. (n.d.). *7 Stages of Grief.* Retrieved February 2, 2017, from Recover From Grief: http://www.recover-from-grief.com/7-stages-of-grief.html